I Am My Body

I Am My Body

A Theology of Embodiment

Elisabeth Moltmann-Wendel

CONTINUUM · NEW YORK

1995

The Continuum Publishing Company
370 Lexington Avenue
New York, NY 10017

Library of Congress Cataloging-in-Publication Data

Moltmann-Wendel, Elisabeth.
[Mein Körper bin ich. English]
I am my body : a theology of embodiment / Elisabeth
Moltmann-Wendel ; [translated by John Bowden].
p.   cm.
Translation of: Mein Körper bin ich.
Includes bibliographical references.
ISBN 0-8264-0786-2
1. Body, Human—Religious aspects—Christianity.
2. Jesus Christ—Humanity. 3. Feminist theology. I. Title.
BT741.2.M6413   1995
233'.5—dc20   94-37801
CIP

Contents

vi   *Contents*

Introduction

Up to the fourth century after Christ, there was a strange monument to early Christianity in the Syrian city of Caesarea Philippi. The church historian Eusebius describes it like this:

> There stood on a lofty stone at the gates of her house a brazen figure in relief of a woman, bending on her knee and stretching forth her hand like a suppliant, while opposite to this there was another of the same material, an upright figure of a man, clothed in comely fashion in a double cloak and stretching out his hand to the woman; at his feet on the monument itself a strange species of herb was growing, which climbed up to the border of the double cloak of brass and acted as an antidote to all kinds of disease. This statue, they said, bore the likeness of Jesus . . . (VII, 18).

This was the cult place and memorial of a healing which is described in the New Testament, the healing of the 'woman with a flow of blood'. Her house and other monuments could be seen here until they were destroyed under the emperor Julian the Apostate as a Christian memorial. Presumably this scene of healing was modelled on cultic depictions of Aesculapius, the Greek god of healing, or had translated him into Christian terms. At all events, for a long time it recalled the unusual healing of a woman who was also depicted in an unusual way in the New Testament – above all in Mark. This passage was never included in the prescribed readings of the church's liturgy. For many theologians even now it is amazingly concrete (thus Schweizer, 117) and as a remnant of magic is thought unsuitable material for sermons. However, nowadays it is again being noticed by theologians (e.g. Peter Trummer), though so far it has hardly been rediscovered as evidence of the centrality of the body in Jesus' message.

I want to begin my investigation of the body and embodiment with this physical story.

> And a great crowd followed him and thronged about him. And there was a woman who had had a flow of blood for twelve years, and who had suffered much under many physicians, and had spent all that she had, and was no better but rather grew worse. She had heard the reports about Jesus, and came up behind him in the crowd and touched his garment. For she said, 'If I touch even his garments, I shall be made well.' And immediately the haemorrhage ceased; and she felt in her body that she was healed of her disease. And Jesus, perceiving in himself that power had gone forth from him, immediately turned about in the crowd, and said, 'Who touched my garments?' And his disciples said to him, 'You see the crowd pressing around you, and yet you say, "Who touched me?"' And he looked around to see who had done it. But the woman, knowing what had been done to her, came in fear and trembling and fell down before him, and told him the whole truth. And he said to her, 'Daughter, your faith has made you well; go in peace, and be healed of your disease' (Mark 5.24–34).

Perhaps more than any other, this healing story, the story of the woman with a flow of blood, plunges us deeply into the dimensions of the body, shows us the body as a field of energy. The words which interpret and confirm what has happened only follow later, as a second stage.

The story is told three times in the New Testament, but only the early version in Mark is so physically dramatic. The later narrators Matthew and Luke already felt the 'painfulness' of this account and deleted its vivid physical features – a process to which the church increasingly fell victim and in which Christianity was robbed of its substance.

So let's keep to the earliest version, Mark's version, here. A woman emerges from a great crowd; we are told that she wants to touch Jesus and his garments in order to be healed by him (Mark 6.56, etc.). This is nothing unusual for someone in Jesus' environment, but her previous history again makes what she is doing quite special. The woman has been bleeding for twelve years. Twelve years – that is not a number which is chosen at random. Twelve years – that is the time a young person takes to attain puberty, and here the time of sexual maturity has been wasted, has bled away, gone. Twelve years – that is also the number of perfection: three times four, heaven and earth together, a time which cannot be surpassed. Twelve – that is again a recollection of the twelve tribes of Israel. Is an allusion to Jewish culture being made here? During this time this woman, who was probably not without means, has been spending all her money on doctors, has 'suffered' under them – a word which we know otherwise from the passion of Jesus – and has come to the end of her tether.

The bleeding, which is not menstrual bleeding but bleeding caused by an illness and which cannot be stopped, is not a disease. It is associated with emissions, odours, impurity; it is disgusting. The term used is 'flow of blood', taken from the Old Testament laws (Lev.15.25), according to which contact with such blood or with the garments of a woman so afflicted makes a person unclean and therefore leads to social and religious isolation. We may imagine the woman to have been married or unmarried, but whichever was the case, she was necessarily isolated from human company.

Biologically, bleeding for twelve years is inconceivable. It means death, and in every respect of her life, economic, psychological, religious, the woman is really already dead.

There is a modern parallel story by Marie Cardenal in which a young woman describes her bleeding for three years as such an experience of multiple deaths and celebrates her later healing as her 'birth'.

Burdened in this way, the woman is not forward in entrusting herself to Jesus, but comes up secretly from behind. This is certainly no clever trick; this is an emergency. She must also be aware that when she touches him she will make him unclean, but she has shed all her inhibitions. Her conversation with herself, which is unique in the New Testament, 'If I touch even his garments, I shall be made well', is her only support. And through this touching, this direct contact, she is healed. Just as the springs of heaven cease after the flood and the earth again becomes dry and fertile, so here the springs of blood dry up in her. The woman senses, knows, experiences in her body that she has been healed from the scourge which has tormented her. The Greek word used literally means 'scourge'. Here for the second time there is an indication of a connection between the fate of Jesus (at his passion) and that of the woman.

Her blood remains in her. Her strength no longer flows out. Something belongs to her which she had previously been shedding. She is somebody, a body which does not suffer and has to give itself up.

Now interestingly enough this experience does not come from any promises of salvation by Jesus. It is located solely in her body. It is purely bodily well-being. And it is something that she has got for herself. Alone, without anyone with her. Alone, against all the rules and regulations.

The one who also feels something is Jesus. In contrast to her he senses that a power is leaving him, that someone has touched him from behind. He does not know where his energy has gone. But when he makes out the woman in the throng, when she begins to be afraid and to tremble at her terrifying and marvellous physical experience, which for her has become the experience of God ('fear and trembling' are always connected with revelations of God), it is not he who is the active hero of the story, but the woman. She – not he – knows what has happened, and *she* tells him the 'truth', that important word which we usually remember as a term that Jesus applies to himself: 'I am the way, the truth and the life.'

Jesus experiences the truth through her, including the truth about himself and his capacity; he experiences the truth about himself and his body, which is a human body, but full of divine powers, of life-giving energies which he can communicate to others. God is not a spirit. God is there in bodies and their energies, alive and active. Though the story may smack of magic to some enlightened people, it is a physical story, the story of our bodies, which in Christianity have been forgotten: crucified and never raised.

And the truth about this body is also that here it releases forces which make another body healthy, so that here Jesus is in the utmost danger. For he has broken through a whole order which was built up on the logic of the notion of purity: the woman has been healed, the flow of blood has been stopped, and no purification or sacrificial rite was necessary. The healer, too, has set himself above the tabus. It is no coincidence that in Mark this bodily contact between the woman and Jesus, his body anointed for death (Mark 14.8), and finally his dead body (Mark 15.43), are described with the same Greek word *soma* (body), which occurs only in these passages. Thus the story also refers to the Last Supper in which Jesus points with the bread to his life-giving body now given in death: 'This is my body . . .' The life-giving, broken bread is a symbol of this body which makes life possible and is now given over to death.

Since in Christianity the eucharist is always associated with mourning, death and sacrifice, we should read out of the story this bodily aspect of giving life, making healthy and whole, of vitality which breaks through outdated orders.

The interpretation which Jesus finally gives to the story goes beyond an individual framework. What he literally says is 'Go in wholeness – *shalom*.' This really means more than our 'Go in peace'. *Shalom* points to the time of salvation in which it is not just the individual who experiences peace and well-being but the whole creation, all society, all peoples. The way in which Jesus addresses the woman is important for this view. He does not say 'My daughter', suggesting some father-daughter relationship between himself and her; he says to her 'Daughter', and if we look for the origin of such an address we come upon Old Testament expectations, where the 'daughter' of Zion is promised health and wholeness – *shalom* – after sickness and disappointment at the hands of physicians (Jer.8.19ff.; 33.6; Isa.62.11).

The image of the daughter as the people is here seen again in an individual: she embodies the new people of God made up of women and men, which fulfils the hope of the prophets. However, there is no prophecy of a healed world. A way is shown which can be taken in the knowledge that 'salvation has come about in your body'. Nothing can discriminate against it, segregate it, make it painful any more. It belongs to you. It makes up your person. It surrounds you with physical peace, so that you can be sure in yourself that you are yourself. 'I am I.' Liberation takes place in the body.

II

This story makes clear to me how central the body of God (of Jesus) and the human body (the woman's body) once were in Christianity and how they could motivate us, with our knowledge of the loss of our bodies as the loss of ourselves and of the interchange between body and energy, to ask new questions about our bodies in the present.

The body – for many people this has associations of warmth, love, sexuality.

The body – others associate it resignedly with youth and beauty and look on with dismay as their own bodies become older.

The body – this conjures up the daily pictures in the media of murdered, burned, raped, famished bodies, a violence which is spreading to our streets and schools. The experiences of human bodies have never been as concentrated as they are today: freedom and enjoyment, sickness and a long old age, violence and hatred – all this can be seen and experienced in the body.

Here we have a culture which – with the massive support of the Christian churches – has constantly repressed the body and excluded or devalued all that is fleshly, bodily, material. In contrast to Eastern cultures and religions, the Western dualism which divided body and spirit, body and soul, and drew its spiritual capital from this division, has allowed no loving relationship with the body. But what has been so long denied is now seizing by force. The body has become a key theme. The cult of the body is pleasant and has become almost compulsive, and women above all do not hesitate to use every means and take great efforts over it. Body language, workouts, body therapy are notions which have entered our everyday life; underlying them is an approach to a topic which previously had been almost illegitimate. But at the same time a culture of the body has arisen which with, for example, its pornography of violence is more repulsive than attractive and which for many people is again making the topic of the body tabu.

However, what is communicated today from limit situations is important: those who look after the victims of torture report how the suffering of the victims is engraved in their bodies, as the body never forgets. Those who deal with women who have been abused know that the humiliations make it very difficult for them to have a new feeling of self-esteem. Who already knows today how women's bodies, exploited and investigated by all kinds of research, react to such misuse?

The body, for long a scientific object, matter to be treated and dominated, proves to be 'terrible' and 'remarkable' (Alves). It is a new continent to explore, a mysterious microcosm, like the macrocosm earth which has just been rediscovered – self-organized, 'intelligent' and mysterious, something that we cannot approach as an object but of which we ourselves are always a part.

Perhaps today the insight of Viktor von Weizsäcker, who called for broader perspectives on what happens to the body and a much wider reference to the environment, is beginning to become established. He thought the 'mystery of the body' much greater than that of the psyche and saw here one of the main defects of Freud's conception. Today anthropologists like Rudolf zur Lippe are asking whether it is not time to investigate the deep physiological strata to which the strata of the psyche are bound (Kamper and Wulf 1982, 36). The interest in the psyche which governed the first half of the century is shifting into physics. Some psychotherapy has become bodily therapy with a psychoanalytical orientation. The 'return of the body' – envisaged ten years ago – is now beginning to take shape. Above all from women's studies, voices are being raised which call for thought from the body and see the organism as the origin of all reflections (Naomi Goldenberg, 184ff.). New light is being shed on the body as the place in which many processes are articulated and as a primal experience of the way in which we are all interconnected.

But the topic of the body confronts us above all with the distinctive character of the Christian tradition: God's becoming body. This was already scandalous in antiquity and is still inconvenient, and its significance for society, cosmos and the individual has hardly been worked out. Deaf to such questions, some churches even persist in a hostility to sexuality which is no longer viable.

In this book I want to investigate the body, its experiences, its traditions and its religious and social significance, without bringing sexuality, which from the male perspective is still the central topic relating to the body, into the foreground. Nor will menstruation, the female equivalent of coital sexuality, which today is the starting point of many women's experience of themselves, become a focal point of my reflections on the body. For the topic of the body comprises more realms than such narrow perspectives allow. However, individual topics like handicap, incest, rape, which are only alluded to here, need a separate investigation.

The topic, with its varied social, medical and cosmic associations, compels us not to keep to a neutral approach; it calls for involvement. That can be annoying, but it can also be a motive for becoming open to new areas.

Stimulated by feminist practice and theory and by feminist theology, I shall begin with the experiences that we have of our bodies as men and women in a society which is constantly changing but which is still stamped by the values of Western Christianity. These are experiences of childhood, of youth, of sickness and of growing old. In the second part I shall investigate the ambivalent role of the church and Christianity in this process: it is ambivalent because the hostility of the church to sexuality is paraded before our eyes every day, and also because Christianity has an affinity to the suffering body which is unique in religion. It is also ambivalent because women's bodies are feared and denied, and yet the healing of the whole person as woman and man was the centre of the Jesus movement. How can we regain this sense of the body? In the third part, 'Being Open to New Areas', I shall indicate the beginnings of a new orientation on the body which is making women autonomous in both their senses and their understanding and is leading them to break open old vessels, which is bringing our thought closer to life and the body, and which could create liberating relationships for women and men: spheres of life which we need to develop our powers of life.

At the end of this study I have brought together some 'Thoughts on a Theology of Embodiment'. The body and its rediscovery could prove to be a turning point in our Western development. As a theology of embodiment, theology, which I understand as a living interface between Christian Western traditions and liberating social movements, could pose new existential and social tasks and communicate wisdom and knowledge as an inseparable unity. There are the beginnings of 'embodiment' in some theological approaches, e.g. those of Walter Hollenweger, Richard Rohr and Rubem Alves.

However, not enough attention seems to have been paid here to the feminist aspect, though that is urgently necessary at a time when women's bodies are being violated in new dramatic ways. It compels us to take a new look and understand the whole extent of disembodiment, of hatred of the body. The title of this book is *I am my Body*. That is not meant to indicate some revival of Western individualism in a feminine form. It refers to a self which is bound up in this multi-dimensional body and which experiences relationships and selfhood through it.

The discussions in each chapter are self-contained, so that each can be understood on its own.

I am grateful to Ingrid Adam for technical advice; Ali Mausshardt and Jürgen Moltmann for technical advice, for their critical reading of the manuscript and for important suggestions; and to Dieter Heidtmann for his attentive reading of the proofs.

I

Our Body – Our Self

Continence heals the sinful body.

(*Trithenius von Sponheim*)

Our body loves us, and even while the
spirit is dreaming away, it is working
to remedy the damage that we do it.

(*John Updike*)

Having a body – being a body

Our predominant experience is that we *have* a body. We have a body
for working, for running, for carrying, for loving, for eating, for
dancing, in short for doing all the things that we have to do and like to
do. Our predominant experience is also that the body functions, that
it does what we want it to. When it no longer does so, we become
insecure. We lose the rhythm and the framework of our everyday life.
If the body no longer functions, we no longer function. We go to the
doctor and take along our body for repairs. Perhaps we have a guilty
conscience that we've neglected to have an annual check-up and are
relieved when the body gets going again, just as we do when the car
has survived its annual test. After such experiences we determine to
treat this precious and dear instrument of our life more carefully.

If the body begins to stop functioning, we make those around us
insecure. And in such crises we have another experience, namely
that we *are* bodies. The instrument which copes with life and gives
pleasure in life gives us another experience: that it is our prison. If we
are sick, unwell, tired, have a pain – we get blocked. The body takes
over our will, our understanding. Now it no longer begins below the
head, but is the whole of us. We *are* bodies.

This experience is important. Unhappy though it makes us at first, it is central to a happy and successful life which does not suppress the dark side of life and escape into a disembodied world of concepts and the spirit. 'Without this body I do not exist, and I am myself as my body,' remarked the Russian philosopher Vladimir Iljine. However, this experience of being a body cannot be taken for granted in a competitive and consumer culture in which people think that they can have all the achievements and pleasures they want. Unfortunately we only learn that we are bodies – painfully and in a limiting way – in boundary situations: in chronic illnessess, in handicaps which seem final, in old age, when there are no longer any fountains of youth to promise eternal youth. The journalist Vilma Sturm anxiously noted in her diaries: 'The body, this head-trunk-two arms-two legs-body – what a reliable companion it had been! It moved and stood up and ran, it carried and hauled, it jumped and turned in the dance, it swung over parallel bars, head up, head down. It swam and rowed. It threw and hit the ball, had the strength to dig the earth. It could not do everything, but at least it did most of what one expected of it; it was at one's service, did not have to be asked for long. She has already almost forgotten how it was when it simply obeyed her, when she could be sure of herself. Now insecurity, total unreliability, prevails . . .' (Sturm, 48).

The threatening feeling develops that the body is now directing instead of reacting, as it used to. The experience of being a body can be threatening for many people.

However, had we not been brought up to make our bodies instruments, being a body could be a happy experience. Being a body can also be the experience of well-being, of being alive, a conscious experience of the rhythms of the body, the happy feeling of being one with nature, with trees, grass, cats. It can also arise from pleasure and not just from pain. But the church and culture have made pleasure suspect to us. A child has this sense of the body, and it is the upbringing and culture of our society which distances us from our bodies and teaches us to control our bodies. Many adults have to rediscover that they are bodies through forms of therapy. The question is how far this is successful, and whether it does not remain a bit of cosmetics for a disembodied society. We have lost more than we imagine.

So at the same time the question arises: are we really so disembodied or even hostile to the body? Offers of therapy come pouring in. The cosmetics industry is booming. The beautiful man has been discovered. Clothing remains loose and no longer constricts us. Children enjoy a freedom unprecedented in our history. Sexual restraint is no longer asked of young people. Almost everyone loves their body, and does it good through vitamins or fasting. Almost everyone is concerned no longer to look like a roughneck or a wood sprite. Weight and cholesterol levels are constant, fashionable topics of conversation. No one wants either to be too low or too high. Our bodies have now become transparent. Many areas of them can be understood, illuminated and measured, and when the information is right it gives us an apparently good physical feeling. We have achieved a measure of outward beauty and visible health which can hardly be surpassed.

But do these bodies which we love, look after, starve, control, trim, toughen by jogging and yoghourt, express our being? Aren't they part of our having? We want a beautiful, young, competitive, attractive, dynamic body, but is that what our body also wants? Isn't there sometimes pressure on the weight that it needs? And that it often takes back again very quickly? Isn't it forced to have a form of beauty which it doesn't express? Isn't it asked to achieve things which are beyond it? Isn't its well-earned and beautiful old age often over-adorned?

We manipulate the body, but what does the body itself want? Are we ourselves in such a body? Insights and experiences are now emerging which dissociate themselves from a purely biological understanding of the body and discover that the body – like nature and the earth – has a dynamic of its own.

Today we need once again to bring together this 'head-trunk-two arms-and-two legs-body', to experience it anew, to heed its voice, which has hardly been heard, and to see it – and in it ourselves – as part of this cosmos. But the cosmos is not just the tree in blossom; it is also the dying tree. It is nature, and it is our society, which we are and which we shape. So when our body is perceived sensitively, it has a voice of its own which cannot be ignored. This voice does not just tell us something about ourselves. It is not just our voice as an individual, as individuals. No, it can become our voice as part of this society. The writer Helga Königsdorf, who worked as a physicist and mathematician in an East Berlin institute, illustrates this. After the revolution she wrote:

> 'My understanding had been asleep. When I rose in the hierarchy of power, not very high, but at least to levels at which the scenery became clear, at which I could only speak my lines – how could I bear this humiliation? – to levels at which people were talked about in a functional language, one day my hand failed serve me, so that I no longer wrote anything down in sessions. My body was more alert than my understanding. It simply refused' (*Wochenpost* 46, 17 November 1989, 16).

But when do people who experience themselves through will and understanding hear such a voice? Usually we detect the wisdom of the body too late. We are not yet used to shaping our lives with it. The American writer Gloria Steinem thinks that it is perhaps also a process of growth and maturity that we do not see the warnings of our bodies as betrayal of ourselves and our plans, but better as wisdom. Steinem sees such wisdom like this: 'If we bless our bodies, they will bless us' (Steinem, 248). We know the word 'bless' from the church, and many people have seldom felt their bodies as they are to be blessed. Can people bless themselves? In other words, can they give themselves riches, fertility, growth and influence? Today we are at a turning point at which we are learning to treat ourseles in another way. In many public spheres we are learning to be no longer just objects, but active, formative subjects. Yet at the same time we are experiencing that our subjectivity no longer means making others objects, whether these others are nature, our neighbours, minorities, or even the body: the network, interrelatedness – those are the magic words which promise us our power and our helplessness, our interdependence and our autonomy. That is how blessing can come and develop.

But so far we have little practice or tradition here.

Society and the body

We are ill-prepared to perceive our bodies and our cosmos together and in a new way. Three movements which have occupied us in the past – and perhaps repelled some people – have at least provided us with some patterns of life and thought that we can no longer lose very quickly. Here I am thinking of the 1968 student movement, the feminist movement, and the New Age movement. At first sight they all seem to have been related to the body, but at the same time they also denied real human bodies for the sake of loftier aims. What have they handed down to us?

The 1968 revolution broke with the idea of men of steel and women who are there to give birth. The ideals of 1968 included the vision that human beings should not prey on one another like wolves. Social conditions worthy of human beings and thus of the body seemed to be envisaged for real human beings in specific situations. 'There is a life before death.' This slogan of French students was the creed of an immediate change to existing injustice.

Beyond Marx's critique of capitalism people again reflected on his notion that 'the abolition of private property' means 'the complete emancipation of all human senses and properties'. Sexual oppression, which encourages the development of neuroses, was attacked. For some groups, pleasure and sexuality became symbols of freedom from capitalism. The sexual revolution which was to extend to the dissolution of civil forms of marriage, and which had hitherto remained unfulfilled in socialism, was overtaken.

But when we look back on this today, we can see that the real person as man *and* woman was soon lost sight of; perhaps it never came into view. Women soon protested that while they were serving as the goal of social change, personally they were continuing to do slaves' work. They also saw that the sexual revolution did not correspond to *their* ideas. They began to develop their own ideas of sexuality, and cut the links with their big brothers. The feminist movement was already in the making.

The deformation of the human body as a result of economic humiliation was only a secondary objection to the main objection against the capitalist exploitation of society. The 1968 revolution failed to take account of the fact that the whole of humankind consists of both men and women. Despite some invasions for the benefit of humanity, the socialist body remained the body to be controlled, even if in some excesses it abandoned this role.

The feminist movement which emerged from the student movement at the beginning of the 1970s began in what was then West Germany with a highly explosive topic, the requirement for the repeal of paragraph 218 of the Basic Law, relating to abortion. But over large areas it remained bound up with the old suppression of the body. In the early years it was stamped by Simone de Beauvoir's school: following Sartre, this school always saw the human body as an obstacle to freedom. In all the striving for masculinity, here the woman remained something like an unsuccessful man, imprisoned in the remnants of her original bodily nature. Accordingly, women could be emancipated only by emancipating themselves from their female bodies. The consequence of this was artificial fertilization, which was also advocated by Shulamith Firestone in the early years of the feminist movement.

Such radical theories got lost later, but the feminist movement continued and continues to be anxious about a lapse into the biological determination of women. Many people feel that the body can imperceptibly snap shut over women again and banish them to home, child-bearing and cooking. Moreover, it is women's bodies that make them prone to becoming victims: at home, in the marital bed, on the streets, and recently once again in war. As a majority of women in society feel that their bodies are humiliated and humiliating, this is no happy beginning for a women's movement. Society must be liberated and changed so that women's bodies can also be free – that is the demand which recurs in many feminist schemes. In the German-speaking world, Frigga Haug has been foremost in her concern with the relationship between women and the body. Her starting point is the sexualizing of the body, which is socially conditioned. In a 'remembering programme' with other women she investigates various parts of the body, for example the legs, to show how women had to display 'style' with their legs; or the hair, the form and colour of which were seen as an expression of sexuality. For her, sexualizing means the subjection of the female body 'to a constant demand to arouse desire' (Haug, 198).

Frigga Haug also criticizes excessively simple schemes relating to women's bodies, for example the famous women's handbook *Our Bodies – Ourselves*, which do not express any consistent insight into the way in which the sexualization of our bodies is socially conditioned. She also rejects all women's notions of the body which could give the illusion of an all too beautiful harmony with nature. For Haug, the only way back to the body is through the fundamental recognition of the way we are determined from outside, by society. For her, a revolution in social conditions is the presupposition for women's self-determination and for the independence of the body within this world. So women's collectives are necessary for any attempt at an upright stance.

This scepticism about the body from the left wing of the feminist critique of domination does not apply to all feminist attempts. But it is characteristic of broad areas of the feminist movement, and it shows that here, too, the body is a sign of a secondary contradiction within the main contradiction: sexism, the oppression of one sex by the other. Women, moved by feminism, fluctuate between scepticism about the body and hope for the body. The predominant feminist theory forbids hope, but the need to live in today's world creates islands of dance, physical work, experience of the body, which explode theory.

The third great movement of our time which is again bringing the human body into view is the New Age movement. It emerged from the ecological crisis and a fundamental criticism and change in the pattern of scientific thought, and brought about a philosophical, anthropological and religious reorientation. New Age thought is no longer shaped by the mechanistic view of the world, according to which nature is dominated by power and knowledge, but by the idea of the universe as a dynamic network of interconnected processes. Its pioneer thinker, Fritjof Capra, understands the world as a total system in which spirit and matter occupy an equal place. Whereas according to the mechanistic and Cartesian view of the world human beings were understood as machines – in parallel to nature – now they are seen as part of the whole, woven into it and bound up with it. There are no solitary beings. Every creature is in some way bound up with all other creatures and is dependent on them. In such communion with the cosmos the human body, too, is no longer just the object of bio-medical techniques. It is seen as a whole. Factors conditioned by a person's environment, psyche, biography, lead to sickness and health. Powers of self-healing are rediscovered. It is not the small cell which is the cause of discomfort or health; rather, these total influences determine our life, our well-being and our sickness.

Energies are again noticed which are to be imagined in the imagery of flow, vibrations and rhythms, and which make up the dynamic structures of the human organism.

The question is whether in the new 'Age of Aquarius', as it is called, social conflicts which still make a painful mark on our present are not being swept under the carpet: the economic exploitation of the weaker, racism and sexism. Thus Capra attaches tremendous importance, for example, to women and the feminist movement, but we find nothing in his work about the social conflicts which are manifested in women's bodies, like violence, rape and incest. Gently and in an old-fashioned way he again brings women closer to nature (the age-old 'identification of woman and nature') and thus leaves open the question of what this totality would look like in men and women. But we may ask why here the Chinese Yin-Yang symbol, which sees male and female as harmony, stands at the place where one would expect conflicts and proposals for a resolution of the relationship between the sexes. Have Yin and Yang liberated women in China? Hasn't brutal physical oppression of women taken place under this old symbol? Here we have open questions to a world-view which hardly touches on reality and real bodies and yet inspires many people.

The three great movements of recent decades have not left us untouched. They have shown us the economic exploitation of human beings, exploitation which they suffer through their bodies. They have inscribed on our consciences the bodies of women as the last whom the dogs bite. They have, finally, once again directed our gaze to the cosmos and from the cosmos back to the body, in order to see it as a living organism, free from fatalistic determinants and developing its own energies. These have become turning points which are making people more critical, more involved and also more liberated.

At the same time, however, under the surface our still-suppressed culture of the body has developed a kind of counter-culture which has celebrated a liberation of its own. It loves and cultivates the aesthetic, sensual and sexual body for which there are no longer any tabus. But how important are tabus, and what laws are needed by a society to protect it instead of to harm it? The pornography laws, which have been liberalized since 1975, are proving quite helpless;

now young people can get without much difficulty what used to be allowed to adults. But the debate on pornography among the women of the 1980s also challenged the public to reflect on its extremely ambivalent pleasure. The consequence was that pleasure cannot be abolished by censorship, even for women, and that in particular women with a lively awareness have their own access to sexual accounts, though these are beyond the violence of pornography. The book by the feminist Benoîte Groult, daughter of Simone de Beauvoir, *Salt on our Skin*, which she wrote at the age of sixty-eight and which expressed the feelings of at least two generations, conveyed this freedom from the limitations of class, age and marriage. The simple love story of a woman professor and a sailor is beautifully written pornography – a sign that there is also another way.

In what follows we shall encounter this social and anti-social aspect time and again.

Women's bodies

If we turn from theories and utopias back to reality, it becomes evident that medical practices and therapies are resorted to predominantly by women. An adviser on questions of marriage and family life reports:

> Time and again it is predominantly women who go to counselling centres, also with their psychosomatic illnesses, although statistically men suffer from these just as much. Now women were always the weaker sex and might complain. Can't they also accuse? . . . Probably no one will claim that they are hysterical. Among many of those who seek counsel I can hear in the background the cries of Cassandra, and many bodies are still haunted by Descartes' remark, 'I think, therefore I am', or Schopenhauer's 'The world as will and idea.' Are we not now to develop here as fellow creatures a more comprehensive kind of person and perception through more experiences of the senses?

Women are seismographs for changes in culture, and their bodies are the places where conflicts become unmistakably evident.

According to the statistics, on average men die six years earlier than women. This can be related to the pride men take in suffering as opposed to women and their 'instability'. But it is better seen as a threatening lack of sensitivity to one's own body.

'Women pay more attention to their bodies,' says Horst Eberhard Richter. 'They also notice symptoms more clearly than men. In surveys women always have more complaints than men, though men are often ill and also die considerably earlier' (Richter, 14).

For many, a woman's body is the embodiment of beauty. But if we look closer this notion is deceptive, since women's bodies differ widely. There is the elegant body of the small gymnast, the heavy body of the pregnant woman and the bowed body of the old woman. Moreover at all times people have had different dreams about the body: at one time it was the baroque, plump, woman's body, today people look for sporting, dynamic figures. At all events, beauty is a diffuse notion, and it arises among those who look at women and is fed by their fantasies. It cannot be assumed that women want to and are able to free themselves from these dreams and their fantasies. But it is to be expected that new attention to their body will also makes them freer in their perception of themselves and more independent from compulsions to beauty. Their dignity does not lie in the imitation of models but in the development of their person. But precisely here there are difficulties today.

Many women feel that they are being torn apart. The chance of entering many spheres of work previously reserved for men, and in addition the need to maintain their traditional responsibility for housekeeping and children, creates burdens which set off alarm signals in the body. The typical modern illnesses of anorexia and bulimia appearing in the industrial nations, which occur almost only among women and girls, are signs that the female body does not fit into this culture stamped by male competitiveness and is rejecting maturity and growth, while on the other hand it is again tormented by hunger and a desire for life.

Perhaps the failure to relate to the body begins very early with girls, so that they either do not want to perceive their bodies and despise them, or experience them as a constant source of discontent instead of pleasure and well-being.

In her book *Jocasta's Children*, the French psychoanalyst Christiane Olivier describes the development of boys and girls, and in so doing comes up against the phenomenon of a deep feminine physical sense of inferiority. Whereas boys with their bodies are desired and loved by their mothers, who are of the other sex, girls, who are of the same sex as their mothers, begin their lives with a split between body and spirit: the girl is loved as a child, but not desired as a male body (Olivier, 45). Sexually, she is not a satisfying object for her mother. She could be for her father, but the modern father is often away from home. Whereas the glint in the mother's eye falls on her small son, according to these investigations small daughters usually miss the glint and the eroticism as a result of which they would regard their bodies as beautiful and desirable. From then on too much emptiness and a longing for fullness dog girls' lives, and that can become the drama of their lives. The dissatisfaction stemming from the beginning of their lives can also reappear in their love affairs. Women often find it difficult to see themselves as good objects of love, even when their partners tell them that they are.

For some women this early alienation from their bodies, which makes them set out empty and hungry on the quest for wholeness, is then combined later with specific social experiences of being torn between unpaid housework involving the body and professional work involving the head, and intensifies their first negative experiences of the body.

Where a 'glint' is provoked – by men or women – security grows. Where insecurity prevails, women allow judgments to be foisted on them which are not their own. Ingrid Olbricht, who is a physician, draws attention to this in an analysis of medical views about women, their bodies, ailments and organs. Women are told that their bodies are unstable, that menstruation is still a dirty and debilitating affair, that their breasts belong to their husbands and children, and so on.

Women who are unsure of their bodies have forced upon them what from a lofty autoritative standpoint is perceived as the right explanation, even if they do not feel that it is the right experience. For many of them, there is an irremediable gulf between the 'right' explanation and the right experience. But women have also already begun to make their own discoveries about their bodies on the basis of their own experiences. These experiences indicate that the woman's body which is always described as weak and delicate is extremely flexible. In a marvellous way it is capable of change and adaptation, compared with the male body, which changes much less. The development of the breasts, menstruation, pregnancy, the menopause, are stages in a woman's life which the body must cope with or, better, in which it has to change and can produce new energies. Women have meanwhile described the creative forces which are set free in the individual phases. The 'wise wound of menstruation' is for many women a time of creative capacities. By contrast – as above all women from other cultures teach us – the menopause can bring a new feeling of freedom from the tabu of menstruation.

Ingrid Olbricht describes the breast as an active and not just a functional organ – like the phallus; it embodies a decisive, important female potency: the capacity to nourish. One difference from male potency is that the breast gives continuously, and not in a jerky outpouring (Olbricht, 148). Nor is anything wasted, as with the emission of semen. Female potency displays a harmonious picture of giving and taking.

But the society which is orientated on competition and consumption also prescribes bodies in which, for example, pregnancy is an unwelcome exception. The numerous sterilizations which women in the former East German states felt they had to undergo to make them available for the workplace are an example of the unwritten power of society and the helplessness of women to preserve their own bodies.

But alongside this, insights are growing which see pregnancy not just as the phase of the fat stomach, which can be hidden by fashion, but also as an important experience of the body. Pregnancy is not just a time of passive suffering, but can also become the 'lived-out criticism of the ideal of an individual who is identical with herself' (Hardach-Pinke, in Kamper and Wulf 1982, 206).

The prescriptions of how women's bodies have to be in the sphere of love, intimacy and partnership, are perhaps the most difficult to change. For many women it is still always the man who determines what and how sexuality should be. But for many women it has proved that sex is only one expression of intimacy and love, and that love includes the whole person. It can relate both to a woman and to a man. It can represent both lesbian love and a heterosexual relationship. This also puts in question the orgasm, which is constantly in the foreground of public interest. In conversations with women the psychologist Anne Wilson Schaef has discovered that sexual intercourse and orgasm are much less important to them than caressing, touching, embracing. For women, sexual intercourse is often not the only aim. It is a means of getting close to the other person. What they enjoy above all is tenderness. Without this, for most of them sex is difficult and joyless. But only women who are sure of themselves and think that their needs are right can make changes here. Where anxiety and uncertainty about their own bodily needs prevail, *he* will continue to set the style. The sexual revolution which filled the media in the 1960s and which was *his* revolution must be revolutionized once again.

Independence in dealing with one's body also includes responsibility in questions of pregnancy. In the end the woman must decide whether a life coming into being can be accepted or a pregnancy has to be aborted. For it is *her* body which bears and has to give birth to the child. It is her body through which she gives it care and security. It is her dedication through which a human being becomes a human being. Help from outside is wanted, but remains unreliable. The Joint Declaration of the Council of the Evangelical Church of Germany and the German Conference of Bishops, *God is a Friend of Life*, has failed to recognize these connections between the personal dignity of the woman, her body and the child in putting the emphasis firmly on the unborn life and giving the woman above all the function of enduring. Here once again the defectiveness of the Christian tradition over embodiment and the woman is clear. As we shall see again below, life is only life in relationship. There is no abstract life.

If on the one hand we are already experiencing a change in the physical self-awareness and self-understanding of women, there are spheres in which the appropriation of the woman's body has taken on violent and technological dimensions which can only be countered by a change in the political situation. Here are three important spheres:

1. *The appropriation of women's bodies by physical violence.* In the industrial nations this is increasing to a terrifying degree at home and outside the home. Rape in marriage is still not a penal offence in some countries. Incest is another crime which is being made public

by the women's movement, usually against girls, and perhaps even affecting one girl in four. Though it was discovered by Sigmund Freud as early as the 1920s, it was rapidly covered up once again with the cloak of bourgeois modesty so as not to endanger the family!

2. *The appropriation of women's bodies by scientific curiosity.* Recently a short book appeared by Barbara Duden, a historian of medicine, under the title *Woman's Body as a Public Place.* In it she demonstrates that the expected child used to be regarded as flesh of the mother's flesh and as a secret gift of God in the darkness of the womb. But modern technology has made it possible to see and analyse the child, and has degraded the mother to a mere vessel; even worse, to an unreliable, dangerous covering. The child has become a foetus or 'a life' which in the views and practices of doctors, lawyers, theologians, mothers, men and the public has been detached from women's bodies and has developed into an object of therapies, rights and theological speculations. Women's bodies are now seen as a system of uterine care! They are the sphere of life of the child which can be inspected and speculated about by all the sciences, and in which the person and status of the woman and her body no longer has any role.

3. *The appropriation of women's bodies as a means of waging war.* This is certainly as old as war itself. Those women who lived east of the Elbe in 1944/5 can still remember it with terror in their bodies, though in the post-war period it was shamefully forgotten and suppressed until it was made public for the first time in a television film in 1992. Today, terror is evoked in the media by a brutal war in former Yugoslavia, in which women have been raped and pregnant women forced to bear children in order to have them brought up later as Czetniks. Here is compulsory conception, which is taking place in history perhaps for the first time. Here is a weapon which is cheaper and more effective than tanks and napalm. Like torture, rape should be included in the Geneva Convention as a war crime.

Years ago, the American feminist Robin Morgan wrote: 'Our bodies are defined, possessed, maltreated, veiled, bared by men, sprayed with colour or used as metaphors . . . Our bodies are objectified and commandeered for male interests. We have no selves even as far as our bodies are concerned' (Morgan, 78).

We can hear the voices of women who apparently have no bodies of their own, and there are women who have undergone experiences of brutal expropriation and only want to live on with their brains and consciousnesses.

One of them writes: 'The body was the body of the man. My body was only an indeterminate area which was waiting to be defined and evaluated by the man who chose it.' And another woman, who had been raped by her father, says: 'I wanted to destroy my body, so that in some way I could only go on living with my brain.'

The way back to the body is a long one, for it is a way along which first the centuries-old prejudices of a male society and a still ever-present sadism must be demolished. It is the way of every individual, and it is a way which will lead to its destination only if many people follow it.

However, two positive things must be noted on this often wearisome way: women of the First World are drawing attention to the expropriation of the bodies of their sisters in the other two-thirds of the world. They are publicizing the suffering of women there as a result of cultural customs (e.g. excision of the clitoris) and colonial exploitation (e.g. sex tourism and prostitution).

What is being experienced here in women's bodies affects whole generations of women there, who have before them a far more difficult road to self-determination.

And a further quite different but important recognition is emerging. Women with their bodies are beginning to have an experience which is continually suppressed in our culture, namely that life is shared life and that it begins with a twosome. As Annie Berner-Hürbin writes: 'We grow in our mother's bodies and at the same time flow into our mothers' field of energy. We may also assume the same thing of the bodies of our mothers which grow around us, the fields of energy from which flow into ours and fuse with it' (59). 'Our life begins in dimensions which transcend the anatomical limits of our body towards an infinite destination from an infinite origin.' The 'empathetic continuum' (Keller, 186) of mother and daughter which is never given up consolidates this primal feminine experience of the body once again, showing that we do not begin as monads but as beings in relationship, who are concerned not to destroy ourselves but to attain recognition and selfhood with one another and through one another.

Men's bodies

Nowadays men are felt by many women to be the powerful sex. But there is doubt whether they really are the strong sex. Initially there are some indications of strength: the physical build of the male is striking. His muscular power is greater and he can do anything requiring this muscle-power, like pulling, lifting, beating, striking, better than women. In competitive sport, which similarly requires muscle-power, he is better than a woman. His heart is larger – it always corresponds to his clenched fist. While a woman's heart weighs 226.8 grammes, a man's heart weighs 283.5 grammes. On average his brain also weighs 120 grammes more than a woman's. A survey has shown that the average man is 1.76m tall, the woman only 1.64m. He weighs on average 75 kilos, while she weighs 63, and his hands and feet are also larger. But the striking differences already stop there. With the exception of the sexual and procreative organs the internal organs are very much the same. Liver, lungs, pancreas display no female or male characteristics. Nor are size, weight and achievement interdependent. Relative to her body, a woman's heart performs just as well as a man's. The greater size of the man's brain has not been conclusively connected with greater intelligence.

When physical power is called for, the man seems strong. But over recent decades investigations have shown just how vulnerable and susceptible he is. Already in the womb he is more unstable: it is male embryos which predominantly perish in the womb. The cause for this seems to be the Y chromosome, which is responsible for the formation of a boy. If a male sperm penetrates a female ovum, the individual chromosomes are connected in pairs to form a new chromosome chain. If the sexual chromosomes pair as one X and one Y chromosome, the result is a boy. If they pair as two X chromosomes, it is a girl. But the Y chromosome is smaller than the X chromosome and it is conjectured that certain physiological susceptibilities and perhaps hereditary illnesses like diseases of the blood are to be explained by this. The decisive step in the formation of the male is taken in the tenth week of pregancy. The genes of the Y chromosomes cause the cells in the small testicles which they have already formed to produce the sex hormone testosterone, which is responsible for the production of testicles, penis and the male form.

After this complicated initial period, as a baby the boy often develops more slowly than the girl. The mortality rate with new-born boys is greater. According to statistics, as children boys are more often ill than girls. Only at puberty do they gain strength and power.

So men undergo a complicated development. For biological reasons (the interior of the body is too hot) their sexual organs, of which they are proud, are visible and vulnerable. Further limitations are that the male has an unstable inguinal ligament, so that men suffer hernias more often than women; they are more often colour-blind and suffer from blood-related diseases; become hard of hearing around ten years earlier than women; and get gout more frequently than women.

These physiological data normalize the image of the powerful hero. But it is not these minor susceptibilities which make him and his body weak. Rather, it is the patterns of behaviour which he has imposed upon himself as a male in male society.

A man takes far less care of his body than a woman. He undergoes physical examinations less frequently. Automobile accidents more often bring men's lives to a premature end. Men commit suicide more often than women.

Heart attacks, cirrhosis of the liver and lung cancer are causes of death which are almost always connected with the male's image of himself. (To the degree that women attain to these male structures and develop the same patterns of behaviour, similar phenomena can also be noted among them.) Men have to achieve, often under stress, and to meet a deadline. The phenomena are similar in every professional group. The man drinks to relax. He smokes to calm himself down. He exists at a remarkable distance from his body. What leads him to do this is not clear: 'What ticks in the man's brain is his gender-specific identity ... that means his male notions, attitudes, fantasies and wishes. He is programmed by his male Y chromosome, by his hormones, by his upbringing, by his traditional role-model' (Norbert Lebert, *Brigitte* 14, 1982).

We can no longer say as easily as we did in the 1970s that one is brought up to be a girl or a boy. There is a complicated interplay of different social and biological factors. The feminist attempts to get boys interested in playing with dolls have failed. The thesis worked out by many researchers under Evelyne Sullerot in 1978 that the brain is a kind of 'sexualized organ', i.e. that the brains of boys and girls, men and women, are organized differently and in some respects function differently – a thesis which provoked indignation among feminists – was not meant to provide a social foundation for a biological classification of women, but was meant to indicate the challenges that lie here (Sullerot, 352). In a changing society in which nature is again seeking her due, the potential capacity of women to have a stronger 'integration between the emotional and the rational aspects of life' is an opportunity to deal on an equal footing with understanding and feeling, head and body. Or better, if possible, we should longer distinguish the two spheres in a way which separates them, and instead attempt to find a total pattern of life and thought. But the Franciscan Richard Rohr complains for all males: 'We have not even idolized the whole head, the whole brain, but only the left half of the brain. According to scientific investigations, the left half of the brain is the analytical side which is capable of thought. The left half of the brain thinks in a polar way: either-or. It does not think synthetically, or in connections. It is incapable of grasping a both-and. The left side is absolute – apparently logical – but in reality ideological. The left side is intelligent, but not wise . . . We must rediscover and develop the right side . . .' (Rohr, 1992, 68).

However, first it seems to me once again to be important to investigate the striking remoteness of the male from his body. This cannot be explained from the weaknesses associated with his origin. On the contrary, because of this he should take particular care of his body. Perhaps the psychoanalytical observations of Christiane Olivier will help us towards an explanation.

In her view the small boy has an infinitely better chance of being felt to be beautiful and attractive by his mother, who is of the opposite sex, than the small girl. This deep erotic love and acceptance give him an assurance which can accompany him through life. He feels good where he is. However, as he must experience later, the tragedy is that he is different from his origin; his body is different; he has to detach himself from the symbiosis with his mother in order to find his own identity. In order to escape his mother's desire, Olivier writes, 'the boy will repudiate everything to do with his body. His body was the attraction for his mother; it stood for everything connected with a sense of life with which it had surrounded him all too much, indeed had throttled him' (Olivier, 94). The mother drops out, and with her the spheres of nearness, nourishment, warmth, motherliness and feeling, which he has to leave behind. And with this loss he leaves behind part of his body, the place of experience and the starting point of these feelings. What remains is a self-awareness which was acquired at an early stage, but remains remarkably detached from the body. Many boys are not at home in their bodies, although they think that their strong bodily physique is a sign of manliness. This physical character which is foisted on them is an instrumentalized embodiment. It demonstrates power and force. For the small boy and adult man it is proved by the erect penis. But behind this is concealed a self which is dependent on such demonstrations of power and can never wholly cope with its separation from the sphere of the feminine, the maternal, from its feelings. This self lives in fear of failure.

The vision of physical strength and power is developed against that: the vision of the father with a powerful body, as Tilmann Moser describes him in his fantasies about a handicapped father (Moser, 69ff.). The vision of physical powers like those represented by the plastic He-Man, Turtle and Batman, dynamic conquerors of the world in the battle against evil, all with inflated chests (exaggerated self-consciousness) and underdeveloped stomachs (a lack of feeling). Moreover, they are all equipped with the most modern weapons, which are apparently meant to back up a physical power which is still inadequate – in the end they are all descendants of the Western Christian hero St George. According to a saga, booted and spurred, with helmet and in armour, riding a horse, he killed a dragon. In our male Christian world we usually understand dragons as embodiments of evil. But if we investigate their original significance, which is still present in Eastern Asia, we find that they are also bringers of happiness, symbols of the unconscious and the feminine. The boy could also have had as ambivalent an experience as our experience of the Western St George today. But the myth of masculinity haunts all spheres. The armour remains, the thick skin as self-protection which lets nothing out and nothing in, and which is further fortified by the managerial training which is customary today.

First of all, the illnesses which are increasingly appearing among males need further explanation. The suppression of feelings makes them hardly perceive their bodies, so that an observer of a male ward in a clinic notes: 'Sick men are like sacks of potatoes, suddenly knocked over by a magical hand.' The 'suffering of not being able to suffer', as Horst Eberhard Richter terms this phenomenon, absolutely ruins their bodies. The fragile self, detached from its origin, thinks that it can console itself for its doubtful and weak points with its power. But here, too, defeats threaten which destroy its picture of the world. Always strong, always successful, always potent – these are slogans with which many men must struggle from their early childhood days onwards, and in the end these slogans bring their lives to an end six to eight years earlier than those of women. They dream of victory, and for ages victory and death have been part of the lies and deceit of the heroic sagas.

Observations indicate that medical care should pay more attention to men. But here the cat is biting its own tail: those who do not want to be looked after will resist any appropriate precautionary measures. However, a generation is also growing up which increasingly looks self-critically at the idolization of power and strength. Fathers who change their small children's diapers, who do civilian service, who quite naturally look after the old and the handicapped, are images which are appearing increasingly frequently in our society. But the old models of our fathers and forefathers are programmed into our bodies and consciences and take hold of us again if we do not fight against them.

Men who acknowledge their homosexuality similarly represent a quite different life-style: sensitive, and open to their own bodily needs and those of others.

Since I think that the body is the hinge of human personality, we must also begin with the body to find healing and health again. The three great movements which are shaping our culture have not brought men much liberation. The sexual freedom which the 1960s brought with them has intensified the anxiety of the male about always having to be potent. The feminist movement suspected him of being a chauvinist and – in contrast to the penis-envy which Freud claimed to find in women – suggested that he was subject to an envy of giving birth which he did not always want to acknowledge. The New Age Movement required him to reflect on nature, but usually left him with the feeling that this – like everything else in this world –

could be manipulated. His own involvement in this nature, the experience of not doing something but first experiencing, suffering and thus having to change himself, was all too often overlooked. And yet in these three movements there are demands which can make men reflect and find their own way to themselves.

However, a man's body will continue to remain a dark continent to him, which unexpectedly draws attention to itself through discomfort, pains, sicknesses, in which apparently evil, uncanny drives lurk which he thought that he had learned he must control and which could again swallow him up in the physical, feminine, maternal sphere from which he had so laboriously detached himself.

The processes of change are under way, but it will take a long road and many detours before there is any fundamental change.

Parents will be needed who share their care of children in all spheres, so that fathers are involved in the bodily life of their children and this life is no longer fused only with the mother.

Teachers will be needed who no longer preach the dominance of the will over all the other drives.

Women will be needed who put question-marks against male competitive sexuality and show men the whole body, including male bodies, as a sphere of love, tenderness and sexuality.

Friends will be needed who show men a non-phallic embodiment and a life-style which is not centred on the self.

Finally, and above all, men will need to find their own place in a changing world, not in self-pity, but with curiosity.

His capacity for detachment and abstraction, for order and system, could then be made fruitful. It would no longer need to dominate life from above, but could help him to shape himself.

The sick body

'I've a fever', 'my stomach's on strike', 'my back's out of action' – that's how we first perceive our illnesses. We keep them from us, see them as an isolated defect which can be remedied in isolation, until one day we have to say, 'I'm sick.' Then we are saying something that we do not normally say of ourselves: that our destiny is to be bound up with our bodies. In a variety of situations we can distance ourselves from our bodies, but at some point they get hold of us and will not let go. 'I am my body.' Being unwell, fever, pains, restlessness and paralysis preoccupy us. The I, the self, our feelings are surrounded with them. We cannot get away from them. A dark world shapes us, whereas normally we allow ourselves to be shaped by so many more welcome events. It is not only my body that is sick; I am sick. I am in my body. I have no other identity.

Unfortunately it is only in such limit situations that we come up against our real existence, namely that we are in the body. If we are healthy, we are not surrounded by our health – unless we have just recovered from a serious illness and are enjoying health like a new garment. A thousand other experiences shape and dominate us. Many people first learn during the course of their lives that health is the supreme good. Many people take it as for granted as the feet which walk and the eyes which see.

But can I say 'I am healthy' in the same way as I can say with conviction 'I am sick'? Hasn't something long been lurking in me which will make me sick tomorrow? A virus, a bacteria, an unrecognized hereditary disposition which is making a devastating appearance? Perhaps as soon as tomorrow I shall no longer be able to walk, I shall find it difficult to think and hard to breathe. As soon as tomorrow my body can grasp me and take me where I do not want to go.

So perhaps our definitions of health are highly unsatisfactory, indeed controversial. When a doctor pronounces a patient healthy again, the patient must regard herself or himself as healthy because he or she is capable of work and can function. That is the simplest and also the most common view. Sigmund Freud and others also define health as the capacity for enjoyment. At any rate this view is opposed to a notion of the body which saw not only the body-machine but also the pleasure of the body. (But how far the woman's 'capacity for pleasure and enjoyment', not a topic Freud identified, was thought of here remains an open question.)

The World Health Organization goes still further: 'Health is a state of complete physical, mental and social well-being and not just the absence of disease and infirmity.' Fine though this maximal demand may sound, it is put so idealistically as to be problematical. Certainly it is important that any view should no longer consider just the individual, but also the individual's social involvement, which is part of health. It is also important that education should equally be counted as part of the whole and sound personality. But this notion expresses the dream of a healthy society rather than indicating a practicable vision of health. The questions raised by this definition are: Doesn't it overestimate the physician or ask too much of doctors? Isn't there also a need for some kind of psychological and political therapy in the medical system? Isn't the basis of the definition a utopia of immortal, eternal life, a utopia of life without suffering, of happiness without pain, of a society without conflicts? At the least it is a definition which fails to do justice to the human body, which is never perfect, which ages, becomes sick, is part of society, and precisely in all these imperfections can experience happiness and well-being. This definition from the perspective of the left-wing critique of domination ultimately, like the critique itself, leaves the body in a corner as a reflection of society.

The formulation of the Christian Medical Commission of the World Council of Churches is almost even more idealistic. It states that health is a 'living sign of the well-being of the individual and society, of bodily, spiritual, mental, economic, social and political stability'. Health is harmony with oneself, with one's fellow human beings, the environment and nature, and with God. In the right context health is *shalom* = peace (Isa.32.16f.), a sign of the correct interplay.

If we want to find words for 'health' at all, then Ivan Illich's approach is nearer to reality. For him health means 'the process of adaptation, the capacity to adapt to a changing milieu, growing older, convalescing, suffering, expecting death'. Health is then 'the capacity to overcome pain, sickness and death autonomously,', the power to live with disorders or health is, as Karl Barth said with reference to the psychosomatics of Richard Siebeck, 'the strength to be human' (Moltmann, 273). However, these definitions 'autonomy and power' need a further addition which male contemporaries easily overlook. Autonomy needs relationship, and the power to be human is nurtured, consciously or unconsciously, by relationships. It is one-sided confidence in one's own power that makes one sick. That is what lies behind heart attacks. Health – if we want to define it – is indissolubly connected with relationship and concern. Stress and death arise through isolation. As experiments with animals also show, loneliness has a direct effect on processes in the brain. Health then means living in oneself, with oneself and in relationships.

But let's return once again to sickness, to the sick body and the terror and pain which it causes us. There has been too much talk about the meaning of suffering, although to those involved in suffering this suffering seems completely meaningless. We should forget this consolation. Sick people can more credibly speak of their sickness as a journey, the 'journey of the poor', on which they have unsuspected experiences with their bodies. After a cancer operation Maxie Wander wrote in dismay: 'I have grown old in an autumn, I have a body which has been cut and which will never again attract a man. Never again will I be able to undress easily on the beach. My body which I loved is mutilated for ever. I can't understand it, it is too cruel . . .' (Wander, 1980, 72). But six months later we read: 'And when life is cruel to you, don't grumble, don't cry, but hold on and wait patiently until something good happens to you. How will you become a human being without pain? It seems to me that at the moment God is nearer to me than to you. You may perhaps want to grasp him with the head, through the understanding, but he shows himself to you in quite a different way . . . Words do not express approximately what I feel is happening to me. But I am just beginning to live . . .' (ibid., 173).

An impressive collection of stories about sick women, *Sickness as an Experience*, depicts such 'journeys' through the fear of death and despair. In it there is a recollection of a remark of André Gide's, that illnesses are keys which can open certain doors to us: 'Among those who enjoy perfect health I have never met anyone who was not in some way a little limited, like those who have never travelled . . .' (Möhrmann and Würzbach, 258f.).

Women with life-threatening, mutilating, wearisome and tormenting illnesses were invited to write their stories. What came out of them, for all the terrible differences, was a help to others. These women faced sickness without compromise. A women tormented by dermatitis was finally able to accept her sick hands again. She had become one with her body, and never again did she have the feeling that her hands did not exist. The stories also draw urgent attention to the fact that concern and love give rise to this journey and that in a sick body a self can establish itself which supports itself and endures itself and finally discovers pleasure: pleasure at enjoying little things and the present, pleasure which quite unexpectedly restores a unity with the body. Something that is never experienced in health comes through pain. What a grotesque detour! A women expresses this being-with-herself like this:

> I feel that the withdrawal into myself during the last months has created a home in me into which I can always go with a light step to withstand pain, to rest or to look happily out of the windows. This little house was already there in the rough during my youth; I kept building on it, and now it is being renovated. The inside is still incomplete, but it can become richer and more varied through experiences and encounters. The old rubbish must be thrown out. There is also a dark cellar of anxieties which I ought not to enter if possible or, better, on which I should shed some light. I keep wanting to get out of the house and receive guests . . . The lack of protection in my life which initially seemed so cruel has extended to become an undetermined but also hopeful possibility. Most of it must come from myself, and for the moment I am up to that. I resonate in myself and let others resonate with me or even away from me. I can roll up into myself, gather strength and turn to myself. There are pains and there is my new joy (49).

This is a sense of life which does not triumph over the body, but experiences its limitations and opportunities in the body. A man ill with Aids put this being at home in the body, almost triumphantly, like this: 'I feel that my body is no longer just a covering, but alive and strong.'

As a handicapped person, Ulrich Bach has said something specially for handicapped people, but which is similar. 'They want to be recognized, recognized in the way in which under *their* conditions they attempt to shape their one life as something precious' (Bach, 202).

Not everyone makes such a journey to such experiences. But the door into new spaces is there, and it can be opened.

Growing old

In a fitness centre a young woman was working out vigorously with dumbbells. When a reporter asked her why she was doing this, she replied, 'To cheat old age.' Growing old and old age seem to be frightening in our society. People think that they can avoid old age like an infectious illness, like a dangerous bacillus, and will try anything to do so: sport, clothing, diet, operations which are supposed to restore youthfulness. Youth and youthfulness has always been attractive. Fairy tales tell of fountains from which people get eternal youth. The Bible promises healing, 'that you may be as young as an eagle' (Ps.103.5). Social groups like political parties, church conferences, societies and churches take great pains over youth. As a report on the elderly in the church puts it: 'The greatest pastoral efforts are directed towards addressing and reaching the young and young adults.' All are striving in their own way to cheat old age. If a person, an institution, is surrounded with youth, that is to their credit and they gain a feeling of self. But the old are there, and old age comes inexorably.

But what is old age? What is growing old? We cannot escape it, as we can escape some illnesses which make us anxious, unless we die when we are young. And the fear of old age has made some people wish for an early death.

Let's look closer at the body in old age, its biological processes and the prejudices attached to it.

Old age is not an intermediate stage like an illness, but is part of the law of life like birth, growth, procreation, death. Old age and death begin when a predetermined programme of growth and maturity has been completed. In old age the tissues change; the mass of metabolic tissue diminishes, while the inactive tissue, e.g. the connective tissue, increases. The capacity of cells to renew themselves diminishes notably. Important organs regress and their functions become weaker. Biochemical changes take place. The hair becomes white and thinner, the skin develops folds. The skeleton changes. The shoulders become narrower, the pelvis often broader. Muscle loss and sclerosis lead to difficulties with walking. The heart does not work as well. The arteries calcify. Less blood flows through the brain. The motor nerves no longer communicate stimuli so quickly. Long-sightedness increases. The sexual organs regress.

But this horror scenario should not terrify us. How quickly individual changes become visible depends on a person's standard of living, level of education, surrounding culture, social and psychological environment. In the rich industrial nations people have greater possibilities of leading a 'normal' life despite the reduction in their bodily functions and can compensate for the decline. Nor does aging occupy a fixed period. There can be a great difference between a sixty-year-old and an eighty-year-old. 'I'm getting old,' a thirty-year-old can say. And perhaps the process of aging already begins on the first day of life.

The body is the terrain on which this process is played out, and particularly in the rich countries the aged body has become a spectre, a spectre contrasting with the ideals of these countries with their self-images of health and success. The disappearance of smoothness, strength, lustre unsettles people and makes them look out for other ideals. That increases the market value of the young body and at the same time makes the old embodiment of the body, the woman, a special terror.

First let's look at how men grow old. The image of the old man has few negative associations; with men age is often associated with status. God is also often depicted as an old man with a white beard, as are Moses, Abraham, the Germanic god Odin, and Vishnu the Hindu god.

Experience, wisdom and authority are associated with masculine old age. By comparison, physical morbidity fades into the background. *The Old Man and the Sea*, the gripping story of Hemingway's own aging, shows victory despite annihilation. The great fish that the old man catches ultimately becomes the prey of sharks. In the end, only a skeleton is left. But the author's conclusion is: a man can be annihilated, but not conquered.

Masculine aging preserves a touch of victory despite the outward collapse. 'Masculinity,' writes Simone de Beauvoir, 'is not a prey to old age' (de Beauvoir, 291).

Things do not look so positive on the woman's side. Brecht's story of the disreputable old woman who after the death of her husband takes out a mortgage on her house and happily gives away her money, falling in love with an old cobbler, and being disowned by her family, was for long a solitary revolt. At the end of the 1970s, Bernhard Sinkel's comedy film *Lina Brake* produced a new type of old woman: an old woman, apparently powerless, tricks a bank, and tricks her own declining strength with a tricycle on which she asserts herself in the traffic. The actress Lina Carstens became the symbol of the coming 'grey panther' with her peaceful and obstinate face, grey bun and old fashioned handbag. However, in the eighth grade of a high school in which the teacher was collecting associations with the phrase 'old woman', the situation of women was seen more realistically: sick, grumpy, untidy, ugly, carping, cross – that was the result.

The wise old woman seldom appears as the counterpart to the white-haired divine leader in fairy tales and myths, though there are instances (like Frau Holle in German mythology). What we find more often is their caricature, like the witch with her bent body. Some years ago a book of medical advice for couples said this about the wife at the menopause: 'the lustre of beauty disappears, the body becomes unattractive except for trivia'. And in 1977 the well-known professor of forensic psychology, Elisabeth Müller-Luckmann, said in an interview for *Weltwoche*: 'The male body ages more aesthetically. The woman's build is more in danger of degenerating into ugliness.' Bodily images are very soon associated with the idea of the 'old woman', and they signalize decay. 'Man' is seen more easily *beyond* his body, 'woman' is seen *in* her body. But the dream body is the young, smooth, dynamic woman's body, as it is dreamed of by men, which occupies only a very brief span of time in the real life of women. What is taken to correspond to this sexualized body is a male body which – as feminists say – remains presentable, marriageable and loveable to the death. Women have often subjected themselves to these norms, denied themselves, failed to stand by their bodies and often tormented themselves physically and without pleasure to preserve youth and dynamism for themselves and others.

However, compared with the man who remains presentable, marriageable and lovable we have a woman whose body does not show the same continuity. Women arrive at the years of change, the climacteric. The menopause is a physically perceptible change in a woman's life. The monthly bleedings cease. Migraine, hot flushes, fits of sweating and even depressions can develop. This second hormonal change which the woman experiences after puberty ends her capacity to have children; that means loss of prestige in the eyes of those who identify being a woman with the capacity to have children. And for the male who sees her sexuality coupled with the capacity to give birth it also means the loss of the sexual object. In 1903, in his treatise *On the Physiological Imbecility of Woman*, the famous physician Möbius wrote that the woman has only thirty years in which she is 'complete'.

Anyone who is dependent on the verdicts of our culture will suffer from this cold-shouldering. Bodily experiences often go with social changes: the children leave home and a woman who saw her family as her object of love stands there with empty hands and unrequited feelings. However, those who have learned to see themselves differently can see this break as an opportunity.

Pregnancies, which despite all the means of contraception were still often feared, are now no longer a danger. Sexuality can be experienced differently and as self-determination. Biological facts confirm this: the oestrogen level declines during the menopause and the progesterone level rises, and progesterone is responsible for sexual pleasure. Women belong to themselves, and this 'other fertility' can become the beginning of their shaping of their own lives. 'My body has never felt as near to me as at this time,' a woman declared. Another says that she is learning to see her aging face as an 'aesthetic face, characterized by life'. The pressure of norms eases, and a new freedom can begin. Many women doubt whether taking oestrogen enables them to get through this phase better. Research into the menopause is still very incomplete. A woman's responsibility for herself should increase, and that means being given information and talking with others at the same stage.

What about the man? Does he remain condemned to eternal sameness? Researches into andrology are still thin. But the myth of the male who does not undergo a change of life is collapsing. Men also experience similar phenomena to women: hot flushes, fits of sweating, diminishing vitality and loss of potency. According to the Kinsey Report the frequency of intercourse declines after the age of fifty.

These changes are visible and threatening for the male. In

addition the physical changes in them often become professional crises. Young men tread on their heels and violate their sense of being succesful and respected. What the body signals is also signalled by the reason. 'I only felt good when others thought me good,' reported a man about his conscious experience of the years of change. Now he is attempting to feel who he is, to become aware of himself, to shift his self-awareness from other people into his own consciousness . . . 'I find this a very good change.'

For the American researcher Gail Sheehy, the crisis for the man is really even greater than that for the woman, since he feels compelled to achieve something that no living creature has ever achieved – eternal potency. 'The permanent anxiety of failing here' blocks many other powers. The fixation on potency excludes a man from the many other possibilities of care and eroticism. However, for that, mutuality is needed, a new experience shared by women and men. A woman sees it like this: 'Since we women are again seeking to see our bodies as belonging only to us, we can also begin to imagine a new male feeling about the body. When men learn to respect a woman's right to possess her own body, they can also accept gentler relationships to their own bodies. Then the phallus could serve as an instrument of relationship and not as an instrument of subjection' (Keller, 318). Bodily energies could be experienced and translated in quite a different way from what we have so far suspected. An awareness of the senses could help men in their ways of seeing and thinking.

So the years of change are years of change for both men and women. However, men still feel less affected by them; they are less informed and more distracted from themselves and their bodily processes by their work. An Abyssinian woman put it like this: 'His life and his body are always the same . . . He knows nothing.'

One important experience could grow out of women's experiences, to help us to understand aging better: that our bodies and we ourselves in them undergo processes of change which are not only losses of youth, activity and functions but also lead to other new periods of life in which unsuspected possibilities lie. Many people are getting accustomed to dying. Reviving can be something quite different. Women in particular are programmed to such processes.

Unlike small boys, who see the man, the father with his body, as their role model but do not yet correspond to him in size, small girls have no model towards which their bodies can develop. 'The little girl's trouble is that her body is not like anyone's. She possesses neither a sex like her father's nor the distinguishing features of her mother (who has breasts, comes in at the waist and out at the hips, has pubic hair)' (Olivier, 46). For women, at a very early stage that means learning change, transformation, flexibility. Menstruation, pregnancy with its immense physical changes and the menopause, are then further phases. They can be endured and be felt to be burdens. But they also bear within themselves the pleasure of becoming new.

Aging could be experienced similarly; as a decline or cessation of particular forces which we no longer need, and as an intensification of other energies we have hardly lived out or active 'passivities' we have seldom investigated.

In her great investigation of old age in 1972, Simone de Beauvoir brought together insights and experiences about aging from the whole history of culture. However, her material was for the most part the experiences of men, since – as she writes – she had not come across many ideas from women and in the 1970s research into women was still in its infancy. This gave rise to a quite depressing panorama of melancholia, injured vanity and repression, as in the case of Richard Wagner, who in horror avoided mirrors so as not to see his 'grey head'. Others complain about the ruin of their bodies, in which their spirits can no longer live. For Chateaubriand, old age was a 'shipwreck'. It seemed to him to be a 'torment to preserve one's intellectual being intact, imprisoned in a worn-out physical shell' (de Beauvoir, 298, 303).

The return of freedom from norms and new openness is seldom noted by de Beauvoir. An Englishmen, John Cowper Powys, is one of the few exceptions here. In his view, in old age people finally come to practise 'that passive activity by which our human organism merges with the Inanimate'. The happiness of old age is to come near to the inanimate. 'There is an inexpressible relationship between an old man warming himself in the sun and a piece of flint being warmed by the sun.' The hardly experienced joys of contemplation could begin (de Beauvoir, 487).

The view of the Jesuit Walter Burghardt is similar. He sees

contemplation as a creative experience of old age. However, for him the way is a *via negativa*, kenosis, a renunciation of what has been had. Here Christian asceticism seems to have shaped a process of thought which then again parts company with the body (*Concilium* 1991/3, 65-71).

Process thought always includes two things, decrease and increase, dying and becoming new. And it is originally related to the body. It avoids the great thunderbolts and is not fixated on breaks. It teaches relaxation or resignation.

Even now, there are few documents by women which reflect on the process of growing old. Susan Griffin has made an attempt. She has described the body of an old woman for us in the style of a biography which is more than the history of an individual life. It is a women's history, which includes all of us and to which we owe our lives:

From the body of the old woman we can tell much of the life she lived. We know that she spent much of her life on her knees. (Fluid in the bursa in front of her kneecap.) We say she must often have been fatigued, that her hands were often in water. (Traces of calcium, traces of unspoken anger, swellings in the middle joints of her fingers.) We see white ridges, scars from old injuries: we see redness in her skin. (That her hands were often in water; that there must have been pain.) We can tell you that she bore several children. We see the white marks on her belly, the looseness of the skin, the wideness of her hips, that her womb has dropped. (Stretching in the tissue behind the womb.) We can see that she has fed her children, that her breasts are long and flat, that there are white marks at the edges and the darker colour of the nipples. We know that she carried weights too heavy for her back. (Curvature of the spine, aching.) From the look of certain muscles in her back, her legs, we can tell you something of her childhood, of what she did not do (of the running, of the climbing, of the kicking, of the movements she did not make). And from her lungs we can tell you what she held back, that she was forbidden to shout, that she learned to breathe shallowly. We can say that we think she must have held her breath. From the size of the holes in her ears we know they were put there in childhood. That she wore earrings most of her life. From the pallor of her skin, we can see that her face was often covered. From her feet, that her shoes were small (toes bent back on themselves), that she was often on her feet (swelling, ligaments of the arches broken down). We guess that she rarely sat through a meal (tissue of the colon inflamed). We can catalogue her being: tissue, fibre, bloodstream, cell, the shape of her experience to the least moment, skin, hair, try to see what she saw, to imagine what she felt, clitoris, vulva, womb, and we can also tell you that despite each injury she survived. That she lived to an old age. (On all the parts of her body we see the years.) By the body of this old woman we are hushed. We are awed. We know that in her body we began. And now we say that it is from her body that we learn. That we see our past. We say from the body of the old woman we can tell you something of the lives we have lived (Griffin, 208f.).

Growing old need not be beautified. Seeing it accurately – without anxiety – makes us see reality, and in it a single liveliness, a single history.

Now for the first time religious images are reappearing which reflect the processes experienced intensively by women: the goddess with her threefold face as a young, middle-aged and old woman is interpreted as women's experience, and in addition is taking on a religious significance for life – of cycles instead of linear patterns which express our life. And the God of the Jewish tradition can also be seen as a woman growing old, who gives a meaning to the rhythms of human life, above all aging. In a sermon, a rabbi in New York tells her congregation how she imagines God:

We become older, as God becomes older. How similar we have become to each other! God takes our face in both her hands and whispers . . . 'Even when you are old I will be with you and hold you when you are grey-haired. I have given birth to you, I carried you, I will hold you fast. Grow old with me . . .'

Our anxiety about the future is now dampened by curiosity. The universe is infinite and still full of unlimited possibilities. And we may welcome every new day with expectant curiosity: what will I learn today, what will I discover? What will I perceive today that I never saw before?

. . .Her face, marked by time, now no longer seems to us to be fragile, but wise. For we understand that God knows about things that only time can teach; that it is possible to survive the loss of a love, to feel certain in a world which is constantly changing, to be able to live in dignity even when every bone hurts . . .

Now we understand why we have been made to grow older: every added day of our life, every new year, makes us more similar to God, she who is eternally older . . . (*Evangelische Theologie* 5, 1992, 382ff.).

God as woman is not only a changed cipher. God imagined as woman creates a broad sphere of life in which our body can be, change and die.

II

The Body and Christianity

The humanity of God is inconvenient

(Rubem Alves)

If one strips God of everything to do with the body,
God is nothing

(Friedrich Christoph Oetinger)

Leaving the body free

The body and Christianity? For many people the associations are
ascetic, denying and despising the body. For many people the body is
associated with sexuality, and on the church's side, down to the most
recent church publications, this seems to be being restricted,
controlled and limited to the partner in marriage. The priest is still
not free to find his own life-style and is obliged to live a celibate life.
In fact the great Catholic standard work of 1963, *Lexikon für
Theologie und Kirche*, confirms such bodily asceticism when it writes:
'The duty to glorify God in the body calls for discipline, readiness for
firm renunciation and curtailment in the sphere of bodily desires . . .
to overcome the flood of bodily drives and the power of sin which
comes from them . . .' (Vol. 6, 905). But even in a more recent
lexicon article (*Frauenlexikon*, Freiburg 1988, 622), the attempts to
arrive at a new integrated embodiment are summed up under the key
phrase 'obedience of the body'. The age-old anxiety of the church
about the structure of human drives, in which it sees sin incarnate, a
structure which is represented in the body and must be tamed by
authority, has still not been obliterated. More recent attempts to
recover a more positive sense of embodiment in the church are
finding difficulty in getting detached from the old thought-patterns

and developing independent ideas which are not just the adoption of modern secular concepts. They would have to bring about a comprehensive change both in the traditional Christian doctrine of sin and in the doctrine of grace. They would have to rediscover the human body as a comprehensive field of energy and as a political organ, and start from the creation, not from the 'fall'.

On the other hand people also have the experience that Christianity more than any other religion practises a broad acceptance of the sick, suffering human body which is despised in many societies. The works of mercy are again the most distinctive potential of Christianity. But what is the explanation of this love of the body on the one hand and contempt of the body on the other?

Is the human body a good creation of God? Or evil, seductive matter which one does better to forget, despise, punish, if need be burn, so that the soul or the apparently immortal part of the person is saved? That is the problem for Christianity.

We shall be investigating this question historically and at the same time existentially. I want to begin from the beginnings of Christianity, the Jesus movement, and trace this remarkable fusion of respect for the body and contempt for the body.

The beginnings of the Jesus movement are stamped by a revaluation of the body. The New Testament scholar Hans Weder thinks that it would have been more appropriate if Jesus had brought about the salvation of the world by 'overcoming his bodily nature' (37). But God became man, became body – as early Christianity saw it – thus raising unaccustomed and explosive questions relating to the religious notions of holiness and women's bodies. However, Christianity did not want in any way to create a new culture of the body. But the reversal of previous values by the preaching of the kingdom of God did not stop at the human body either.

Two phenomena are striking here. First, that healings stand at the centre of Jesus' saving actions. In our church culture and the traditions of its interpretation, above all the Protestant ones, for all too long the word and preaching have been put at the centre of Jesus' action. In our cultural tradition preaching and the word have long been rationalized and separated from the body, so that the church leaves the human body in the lurch. In the Hebrew context in which

Jesus lived and thought, the word (*dabar*) with its powerful energy was still related to the body. Word and healing were indissolubly connected. We who are stamped by an often hollow culture of the word should begin again with the physical process of becoming whole in order to have a new understanding of the centre of the gospel.

Salvation, healing, therefore does not just affect what is within human beings, their souls. Salvation concerns the whole person, since according to the New Testament the salvation of the soul is not yet salvation. The message of Jesus relates to human beings in their totalilty, in their bodies, in which the soul dwells and gives them life. The message of Jesus seeks to change conditions and behaviour which make people blind, deaf, bowed down, paralysed and possessed. It wants people to see, walk, hear and be liberated from all alien determination, including that of the body. It wants to fulfil the Old Testament hope that the lame will walk, the blind see, the deaf hear, the dead rise, the lepers be cleansed, and the poor have the gospel preached to them (Matt.11.5). The reference here is to more than the individual. A society, a community, is being called on to repent, a society from which human beings were cast out because they were sick, in which women had no religious rights, in which relations between parents and children were disrupted. Sin, disruption, destruction becomes evident in human bodies. Even where there is apparently only a discussion with Jesus, the New Testament tells a 'body story': people start on a new way; go off disturbed like the rich young man; come down from a tree (the symbol of the security provided by the mother) like Zacchaeus into an independent life; weep like Peter; find their own language of gratitude like the Samaritan, and so on.

In some stories the healing also take place directly from body to body: thus in three stories Jesus' spittle is the means of cure, the archetype of healing, motherly moisture which recalls the waters from which human beings originate. Whereas other means like blood, breath, oil and wine were used in popular medicine in antiquity, the New Testament tells only of Jesus' own spittle as a means of healing (Mark 7.33; 8.23); in the story of the man born blind (John 9.1f.). Jesus also mixes it with earth, the maternal primal force. The power of healing emanating from the body of Jesus is portrayed very vividly, almost dramatically, in the story of the woman with an issue of blood. The woman grasps Jesus' garment – which means Jesus in his bodily nature – and secures healing for herself.

Theology and the church have long felt such stories about the body to be painful and magical, to be in contradiction to the Enlightenment. They are certainly not coincidental, but were deliberately included in the Gospels and remind us of the forgotten bodily dimension of the message of Jesus.

The second striking phenomenon is that according to the New Testament Jesus, as a Jew, does away with the previous understanding of cleanness and uncleanness. Here he takes up prophetic Old Testament traditions and through them also modifies the levitical laws of purity which regulated dealing with the dead, partaking of food and sexual intercourse. 'He located the contrast betwen remoteness from God and nearness to God solely in the human conscience, and not in the sphere of things' (Wendebourg, 150). Here the woman's body above all seems to be affected; according to the levitical law it was regarded as unclean during menstruation and after birth, and touching it made a person cultically unclean. Emission of semen from a man could also make him unclean (Lev.15.2). But how much more strongly the female sex was affected by tabus is shown simply by the regulation that the birth of a son ceased to make unclean as soon as forty days later, while with the birth of a daughter this period was eighty days (Lev.12.1ff.). Christians could now be charged of no longer 'bathing and purifying themselves as we do' (Epiphanius).

Early Christianity saw itself as being no longer tied to these laws. They had been written down in post-exilic Judaism, but derived from religious rules widespread in the Mediterranean and are to be understood as an androcentric reaction to the early gynocentric, powerful reverence for fertility and blood. So they are in no way specifically Jewish, even if early Christianity thought it had to dissociate itself specifically from the leviitcal laws. The story of the woman with an issue of blood, whose flow of blood is related by Mark to Lev.15.25 and by Matthew to Lev.15.33, shows that with the event of Jesus, with touching his body, sickness was healed and powers emanated from his body which did away with such uncleanness. But the story also shows clearly that Jewish women set this process in motion, since the 'heroine' of the story was the woman, and not Jesus, the miracle-worker.

Not enough research has been done into notions of cleanness and uncleanness in Judaism, the ancient religions and Christianity. Here I can make only a few comments. Women held important offices in early Christianity, and this is hardly conceivable without the abolition of notions of cleanness and uncleanness. But whereas the laws of cleanness which regulated dealing with the dead and the taking of food were permanently dropped, the tabu ideas relating to female sexuality soon returned. Here traditional notions, ascetical ideals, were stronger. This had consequences for Christian women, who, because of their bodies, which were latently regarded as unclean, were in principle kept at a distance from the sacraments, whereas for men abstinence from sexual intercourse was the sole precondition for taking part in the sacrmaent. So women were not allowed to hold the later priestly office. 'Cleanness' – in connection with priests – became the characteristic of the Western churches. Even if other arguments are cited today against the priesthood of women – e.g. tradition – the fundamental objections lay and probably still lie unconsciously here.

But yet another early Christian development concerning women becomes evident. In the Jesus movement – perhaps uniquely in the ancient world – biological social norms were put in question or passed over. This applied above all to ideas about the family. In the Jesus movement, alongside the image of the traditional family there developed the ideal of the *familia Dei*, the family of God, i.e. a voluntary association into which Christian men and women, detached from the ancient blood family, the ancient *oikos*, came together, either for economic reasons or by reason of their faith (Pagels, 20). This family of God understood itself in terms of Jesus' promise that those who forsake all, namely house or brothers or sisters or father or mother or wife or children or land, will find everything again – but no father (Mark 10.29f.). Certainly this sentence says nothing about the woman who leaves her husband – perhaps this was too dangerous for the world of the time – but in the family women could lead another life, free of the compulsions of the ancient household, free from the pressure to give birth. For them that could mean 'leaving the body free', an expression which was

used a few years later by the young Roman Christian noblewoman
Melania who, as a young girl and later as a wife and mother, fought
for this freedom (Pagels, 87). After six years of marriage and the
death of her children she succeeded in leading a life dedicated to
social work along with her husband, because she was a woman of
means. The practices of Jesus' *familia dei* seem to have been the
starting point for a new female life-style which never developed in
such a striking way and so broadly elsewhere in the ancient world.
There were continually groups of women or mixed groups (e.g. the
Therapeutae) in other religious communities which prescribed a
non-marital life-style for themselves. But an 'absolute superiority of
virginity' of the kind that Aline Rousselle observes in Christianity
(Rousselle, 9), was unthinkable in religions orientated on the family.

Such divinely willed virginity could bring liberation in the pre-
modern world from the domination of father, brother or uncle, and it
also promised a new freedom of the body. The renunciation of
marriage and sexuality could mean undivided dedication to other
activities, whether intellectual, charitable or social. It did not
necessarily mean asceticism.

It could also represent continence (*enkrateia*) deliberately entered
into and physical self-determination (Jensen, 110). Only later, with
the institutionalization of this life-style, with the creation of
monasteries in which asceticism was part of the basic order, did the
majority of these approaches get lost.

Alongside the woman of the family, Christianity created a new
female life-style which cannot simply be measured by the monastic
Christian life-style. It had a social significance of its own. It gave the
history of religious women a new accent. It left a trace of bodily,
female self-determination which we should again recall. The
apparently unused biological potential, the powers not used up in the
family, produced spiritual movements, as is shown later above all by
the theological mysticism of the women's convents.

We are accustomed to seeing ascetic women's schemes as hostile
to the body. We should again develop an eye for bodily self-
determination which represents both sexuality in partnership,
heterosexual and lesbian relationships, and also a self-determined
way of dealing with one's own sexuality. The women's movement
has taken up these beginnings in speaking and writing of chastity as

autonomy, of virginal feminism, of ascetic emancipation. Leaving the body freedom is an early Christian programme which we can always follow both as men and as women.

Ashamed of being in the body

But how did it come about that the recollection of an embodiment that makes people whole and sets them free which accompanied the Jesus movement was not only forgotten but could virtually change into its diabolical counterpart? That in the name of Christianity people were tortured and burnt, that their bodies were despised and humiliated, indeed that they hated themselves?

I see two causes:

1. With Paul, who made church history as far as the body was concerned, another way of thinking begins to become established. Certainly he still predominantly maintains the Old Testament totality, but with him *soma* – the body in its totality – and *sarx* – human beings in their fallenness and sin – get mixed up. The high significance of the body for salvation is already constantly exemplified in a devaluation of sexuality characteristic of anthropological dualism (Rom.1.24-27). And these restrictive images of sexuality made possible a pathological church history.

2. The powerful leap which early Christianity made beyond biological and social norms, by seeking to do away with racist and sexist prejudices, could not be maintained. That in Christ there is neither Jew nor Greek, neither slave nor free, neither man nor woman (Gal.3.28), became more programme than praxis. The exaltation of the imminent expectation of the end of the world which had given rise to bold thoughts was diminishing. Reality and dominant society demanded their due. Small, often persecuted, groups turned into communities which were compelled to adapt while retaining many distinctive features, and could not escape the social, ideological and philosophical trends.

The history of the body in Christianity has yet to be written. But we can see three trends which keep recurring and which have shaped Christians' ideas of the body over the centuries:

1. Adaptation to social expectations of the body,
2. The norm of the male body,

3. The acceptance of the body in marginal movements, which has kept breaking through.

I want to describe these trends briefly, in so far as they can still be seen in the present.

1. *Adaptation to social expectations of the body*. At a very early stage, the opportunity to see the female and the male body as God's good creation put Christianity under the pressure to legitimate itself socially. So it adapted Stoic sexual ethics, which saw the significance of sexuality not in pleasure but in procreation – a relic which is still advocated by the Vatican. However, the Jesus movement was shaped by a Hebrew, totalitarian way of thinking which was in no way hostile to pleasure, for which the body was not a material covering for a higher, better soul but was united with the soul as a totality. Under the influence of the Graeco-Roman world view, however, the dualism which thought of body and soul, body and spirit, as opposites was very soon taken over.

This hierarchical view has remained alive in theological thought to the present day, down to Karl Barth, who taught that man is A but woman is B and that the soul ranks above the body (*Church Dogmatics* III.1, 169).

Shame at being in such a lowly body stamped Christian piety for centuries. 'Shame at being in the body' is an expression which Porphyry used of the philosopher Plotinus, and it immediately made history in piety. With the devaluation of the body, woman was also devalued. In the dualistic view of the world there was no longer talk of the equality of man and woman – as in the first account of creation in the Old Testament (Gen.1) and in the baptismal formula of Gal.3.28 in the New Testament. Man was now associated with the spirit and woman with sensuality, nature and the body. In the course of the Middle Ages the 'shame at being in the body' was intensified so that it became a morbid abhorrence of physical processes, taken over from antiquity. And woman was the victim of such hatred of the body. As Odo of Cluny wrote, 'Woman's beauty is no more than skin deep. If men could only see what is under the flesh, they would shun the mere sight of women'. Already in the first Christian centuries, Jesus' friend and the first woman apostle, Mary Magdalene, had been made a great sinner and people had seen their own weakness, sin and failure in her. For example, she was a consolation to Augustine for his own sexual escapades. Now this projection was intensified, and finally the accumulated self-hatred and hatred of women was unleashed in the persecution of witches.

'That home is good in which the man commands and the woman obeys. That person is good in whom the spirit rules and the flesh serves.' That is how Augustine summed up his view of the self and the world, and this view of the self and the world has stamped the West down to our day. At the end of antiquity Aline Rousselle detects a more differentiated situation with three images of the body which mutually condition one another and which similarly continued: the disciplined male body, the female body not allowed to be itself, and the oppressed child's body. The disciplined male body shaped Western history, stamped military training, made industrial society possible and was the model for Protestant social ethics. Today it also fits perfectly into modern Catholic approaches. The body, the sinful body of the Middle Ages, the energy potential of the modern world, must serve, must obey. Its significance lies in being a 'serving body' (Moltmann-Wendel, 1989, 15), not developing an embodiment of its own – a model which can be used by both society and Christianity which makes human beings machines that function well.

2. *The norm of the male body.* When in church practice and theological works people reflected on bodies, it was usually the male body. If women wanted to liberate themselves from their tutelage in the course of history and become independent persons, they had only the image of the male body as *the* valid human body. Already in the early Gospels which were not included in the canon we find passages stating that for women the way to heaven goes only through men's bodies. In the Gospel of Thomas Peter says: 'Mary should go away, for women do not deserve to live.' To which Jesus is said to have replied: 'See. I will take her and make her male so that she too becomes a living spirit who is like you men.' In the church father Jerome we read: 'As long as the woman lives for birth and children, there is the same difference between her and the male as that between body and soul. But if she wants to serve Christ more than the world, she will cease to be woman and will be called man, because we want all the perfect to be exalted to become man.'

In fact for many women the way into the later pastorate was the way into a male profession, orientated on a male pattern of life and on the male body and its availability.

And the universal physical ideal even now is to be thoroughly trained, to correspond to the rhythms of work, trained by jogging and yoghourt. Stress, in order to counter further stress! Two fighting cocks meeting each other! The managerial training which is offered in many places serves to make the body fit and the person psychologically strong. But it is also, as Horst Eberhard Richter says, designed to make people incapable of suffering, and that also means incapable of compassion for other bodies. The male norm of the body, orientated on the rhythm of work, on competition, efficiency and achievement, capable of continuity, is the measure by which embodiment must be guided. Its functionality is the aim and any failure here must be countered.

3. *The acceptance of the body in marginal movements, which has kept breaking through.* Despite all repressions and adaptations, Christianity also always retained the memory of the fundamental acceptance of the body in the Jesus movement. Movements on the periphery of the mainstream churches remembered the body as God's good creation. For example, in Franciscan mysticism the creation was again perceived as God's revelation, and Francis could speak of his body as his brother, albeit brother 'ass', the beast of burden. Hildegard of Bingen avoided all the current dualism of most theologians; she did not regard the body as the prison of the soul, as Plato did, but saw the delightful task of the soul as that of expressing itself in the body and making it an appropriate form. In contrast to the Augustinian hierarchy, her view was that 'the soul supports the flesh as the flesh supports the soul. But each task is carried out through the soul and the flesh.' Indeed, Hildegard was bold enough not only not to devalue the feminine but to see it as 'the primal model of healed and whole humanity' (Gössmann, 118).

In the eighteenth century the Württemberg theologian Friedrich Christoph Oetinger developed a theology of creation in which he proclaimed 'embodiment' as the 'end of all the works of God'. There followed attempts to think in holistic fashion and to overcome the disastrous division of soul and body (Wilhelm Stählin). In the present, theologies of creation have been developed which attach new significance to the human body. However, it remains a fundamental problem that the female body has hardly become the basic model of new thought and action, and consequently one-sidednesses have not been avoided. The male Reformers ultimately went by their own physical experiences without paying sufficient attention to the female body, which in fact makes up half of the human creation. So notions of creation remained divided. The consequence was that procreating. penetrating, separating, knowing and distancing remained the models which corresponded to male bodily behaviour. With them the world and creation were discovered and dominated, and they were projected on to God, to whom one could attribute 'procreation' but hardly 'giving birth'.

Thus female experiences of the body like giving birth, allowing growth, dependence on and participation in nature, the involvement of all with all, remained undeveloped possibilities for action. There was no legitimation for them, nor were there any images of God for them.

So not only was the woman's body left in the lurch. A one-dimensional relationship to the world and the environment developed, the catastrophic consequences of which we are noting only now. Thus the fundamental female experience of the body, that life begins as life together and that the person in relationship rather than the individual should be the starting point of our thought and action, has also remained an alien body in Western theology and philosophy.

The woman's body, the woman with her body, first of all remained suspect, and later became invisible in the church and theology. Her suffering was not noticed; her capacities as shown to us again by nature religions today were not taken seriously. Our being born was overshadowed by our being begotten and brought up. If we want to school ourselves in new thinking we must all, both women and men, bring alive for ourselves the forgotten experiences of women's bodies and introduce them into our world.

The crucified Jesus – the bodily Jesus

What about the body of the central figure of Christianity? What symbolism is associated with Jesus?

A crucifix hangs in almost all churches and in the studies of many ministers as a symbol of Christianity. For many, it is a symbol of the hostility to the body which led Christian men and women to flee from and despise the body. How could a tortured, dying, dead body arouse pleasure and love in one's own body? In fact in Christianity the expression 'body of Christ' refers only to the body on the cross and the risen body. In the eucharist this body given in death, 'Take, eat, this is my body which is given for you', is identified with the bread which is offered. And finally there is the body of Christ in the sense of the church, but this is again grounded in the body of Christ on the cross, which comprises all people of this faith. But is that the whole body of Christ of which the New Testament tells?

We must attack this dense tradition if we want to see the human body once again as God's creation and as a field of energy of unsuspected dimensions opened up to us. We must do this both with our experiences of our own bodies and with a critical approach to, a re-vision of, our tradition. And that also means a re-vision of the life and body of Jesus. Christian theology does not offer a good tradition for this, since it follows the apostle Paul, who did not want to know Christ 'after the flesh' but was interested only in the crucified and risen Christ. But this view was and is one-sided. We have four Gospels – accounts of the life of Jesus – which were extremely interested in his flesh, in his life, and which we could ask about his body and life. They report his birth, his youth, his public career and his death. What is new about our question is that we do not want to ask about his human life generally but to start from the question of his body, which shaped his life like anyone else's: his body – the seat of feelings, the sphere of thought and relationship. Do these old accounts still have something to say for our questions today? Do they fall silent here, or do they give us new insights into the person of Jesus and a forgotten Christian message?

At first it was difficult for the early Christians – as it still is for Christians today – to understand Jesus' birth. Only the first evangelist, Mark, assumes a normal human birth and sees a kind of adoption by God first taking place through Jesus' baptism. The evangelists Matthew and Luke imagine that Mary became pregnant through the Holy Spirit, that her fiancé Joseph was frightened to death at this and on divine instructions was obliged to marry the mother of a child which was not really his. For them, a Son of God could not be conceived in the normal way. This view later began to become more and more established, and today is even to be found in the new *Catechism of the Catholic Church*, in which Jesus also may have no physical brothers and sisters, thus distorting some of the incarnation of God. The Gospel of Mark, which does not yet know such constructions, is also more human in its depiction of the humanity of Jesus than the later writers.

But Luke also relates human features: that after his birth Jesus was wrapped in swaddling clothes, in other words, he evacuated himself like other human beings; and that he was laid in a manger, the image of poverty and for later interpreters a prelude to the cross: the wood of the manger is also the wood of the cross. The later popular notions, which also appear in the mediaeval visions of Brigitta of Sweden, that Jesus lay naked on the naked earth, are much more earthy and emphasize Jesus' humanity more: here is a reminiscence of the powers of earth and the old earth mother, which communicate a physical life-force. Or there is the notion that he was born in a cave, i.e. in the depths of the earth. The picture of the saviour who 'springs from the earth', as in the Advent hymn 'O saviour, rend the heavens', recalls his earthliness and bodiliness.

The human Jesus of the Gospel of Mark also shows very marked human reactions which the later Gospels have skilfully retouched. He is annoyed at the disciples (9.19; 8.17f.) and the Pharisees (3.5), and has outbursts of anger. He groans and sighs (8.12). He welcomes children and does not just use them as teaching illustrations (9.36; 10.16). He is full of compassion (1.41) and loves the rich young man with a love which does not come from above but is mutual, agape (10.21). It can also be said of him that he needs a cushion in the boat to sleep on (4.38) and that his family thinks him crazy, a ne'er-do-well (3.21). Mark also reports his desperate feeling of godforsakeness on the cross (15.34). These are images which show Jesus as vital person, needing company and tenderness, but also capable of passionate outbursts. Here is a Jesus who has a body, and the author of the Gospel of Mark has no problems about that. It is from this body – and not from his will, his head or his spirit – that the energies which heal the woman with the issue of blood emanate (5.30). Though a generation of theologians whose perception was reduced by the Enlightenment may have eliminated such details, we are again discovering them as central christological statements. Jesus is no Gnostic hero who brings us a change of consciousness. He brings liberation from social compulsions and healing for destroyed bodies. With his body Jesus is also drawn into the cosmos: in his anxiety in Gethsemane he falls on the comforting mother earth, which at the same time swallows people up (14.35). This earth quakes at his death and gives up its dead (Matt.27.52ff.). He came into this cosmos – according to the Gospel of John – to heal the divisions of the world (John 11.27).

With a balanced Jesus who could no longer be passionate, angry and tender, it was also forgotten that Jesus lived in and by relationships. Because he was always put on a higher level than other human beings, there was a failure to see that he needed other people for his development, and that the relationships necessary for a person of flesh and blood were also necessary for his spirit and its energies. In relationships we experience acceptance and gain detachment. Relationships are shaped by conflicts and their resolutions. And we experience these with our whole persons.

Jesus' conflict with his family also extends unmistakably into the stories which have been handed down to us. They wanted to see Jesus as a normal 'citizen' and family man instead of as a revolutionary and a single person. And the group of disciples which he then joined did not give the resonance that he needed. These men in love with success disappointed him time and again. He found acceptance, stimulation and new life-styles later with the women who stayed with him to his death, one of whom showed him his way to the Gentiles (Matt.15.21ff.) and another his way to death as the anointed king of Israel (Mark 14.3ff.). He did not understand his life as that of a husband and father, obedient to the family tradition and bringing up children, but as that of a man who devotes body and life to other values.

To this degree his notions of sexuality differed fundamentally from those of his environment, in particular from those of Judaism, as Elaine Pagels has shown (Pagels, 9ff.), though he did not make his life-style a law. But the later Gnostic Gospels relate that he had erotic needs. According to these, Mary Magdalene was his friend, with whom he passionately exchanged kisses. So for him love was not reduced socially to love of the neighbour. He reproaches the

Pharisee who had invited him to his house for a cold and loveless meal. By contrast, the prostitute who suddenly burst into this male circle deeply moved him physically with her anointing. For him, her tears, her hair, her kisses were physical love which gave his body pleasure (Luke 7).

It is also striking what value the story of Jesus attaches to eating. The New Testament meals are too often immediately associated with Jesus' last meal, the Last Supper. But all the meals in his life must have been eaten with enjoyment: fish, lamb, bread, wine, herbs do not indicate asceticism. And the fact that his opponents spoke of him as a 'glutton and winebibber' only confirms that he did not live his life grimly, but in a relaxed way, as a celebration. How parallel his own suffering, life and death were seen as being to human suffering and recuperation in the early period of the church is evident from many terms which can be found in the healing stories and in the passion narrative. In particular the story of the woman with an issue of blood seems to have been understood as an exemplary passion story. The word 'suffer' is used both of the woman who suffered under the physicians and of the suffering of Jesus (Mark 5.26; 8.31; 9.12). In Mark the blood is both her and his blood; similarly, in Mark 'body' occurs only in this story and in the passion narrative. The word 'scourge', used to describe the woman's affliction, is also used in connection with the torturing of Jesus.

In these stories, Jesus' death is still seen in parallel to other human suffering and dying, in which at the same time the power and healing force of God are visible. His dying is still not sacrificial dying for human sin. Here with his uncompromising life he still fought for the life of others.

Later this suffering was no longer seen in the context of human suffering. The idea of representation was replaced by the notion of the atoning sacrifice which had to be offered for the sins of humankind. In this way his death came into a religious dimension which no longer allowed any comparisons with human suffering. Thus his body was distinguished from other human bodies and became the body of crucifixion and resurrection, which had virtually no relationship to his earthly life. His body was seen as a sacrifice which now had to draw other sacrifices after it: male sacrifices in war and female self-sacrifices.

For many people the question will remain whether as God's Son Jesus did not follow other laws, and his divinity is not to be compared with our humanity. I think that his deepest humanity makes up his divinity. As God became human – 'clad himself in our poor flesh and blood' as Luther said – we can all freely seek Jesus' forgotten body. God and humankind encounter each other in the body. God encounters us in the human body. Those who fail to see their bodies fail to see God. The crucifix, which confronts us only with the tortured and dead body, misses the whole message of the gospel.

The body and the church

How does the church deal with the human body? Has the Jesus tradition been preserved, which understood salvation as the healing of the whole person in the body? Have not the later notions of sacrifice which clustered round the person of Jesus led to a negation of the body?

Experiences differ. On the one hand many people experience the church as the place where the weakness and helplessness felt in our bodies can find expression. The Jesus who appears in the hungry, the prisoners, the naked, the sick, as the parable of the great judgment of the world shows (Matt.25.42), has always been a challenge to discover social weaknesses in society and to commit oneself anew for the disadvantaged.

On the other hand, however, many people are aware of the ways in which Christianity distorts the body, and this already begins with the rituals of the church. Penned into the pews, Protestant Christians above all experience that in worship their heads, their ears or perhaps their wills have been addressed, but nothing else. Unfortunately isolated hearing also leads to fatal obedience.

For some people prayer with closed eyes seems like a flight from the world. 'It is remarkable,' writes the Latin American liberation theologian Rubem Alves, 'that we close our eyes to pray. Anxiety about the body? Are we fleeing from the body . . . ?' 'We close our eyes and look inwards – in search of a spirit. But the spirit of God is in things, in bodies, in creation and above all in the laughing and weeping of children and those who suffer.'

For some, tasting the eucharistic bread or host is an almost painful act. While Jesus ate a proper meal with his disciples, all we have left is passive reception, without our bodies being much involved. Where apparently only a spirit without a body is to be fed, the body will also find it painful and do better to remain outside.

Apart from the ups and downs of sitting, standing and kneeling, all that is left as an initiative of the body is singing.

With music and singing above all, Protestant Christianity has for centuries preserved some emotion, pleasure and bodily action in its church. The throat is the organ of breath and the expression of all feelings and senses, and it is becoming clear today that music could to some degree conceal the lack of bodily involvement. But the eyes which in former times found stimulation in images, colours, altars, have had to look inwards. The nose which found a distinctive attraction familiar to many in Catholic incense now no longer finds any smell. The taste of wine and bread was associated with so much anxiety about doing something 'unworthy' (I Cor.11.27) here, that we can describe Protestant church culture as a rabid, rationalistic suppression of embodiment.

In Catholic church culture smells, colours, images and movements are still strongly integrated. But to the degree that they have been so rigidly ritualized that they do not satisfy the present needs of the body, questions remain.

How lively, physical, sensual – and thus meaningful – Christian worship could be is shown by many new forms beyond the structures of our mainstream churches, e.g. at church conferences. Prayer with open eyes and open palms, meals which are consciously savoured, addresses to which people can react with shouts, clapping or even whistling, the kiss of peace, music which not only touches the ears but moves the body, dance which expresses religious experiences and relationships with others, are promising beginnings of a new church which is again finding its way back to human embodiment.

However, it would be unsatisfactory to take over new forms and to leave the basic Christian theological pattern which produced the old forms unclarified. We must be clear that our ritual hostility to the body is deeply rooted in the hostility of the church to the body. It is argued today that the church lacks and always has lacked an approach to eros, but that the positive attitude of Christianity to the body is not affected by this. However, this is to split eros from the body and to see the body only as an object of compassion or an instrument of relationship.

The basic church pattern is shaped by the view that human beings are sinful. There is no objection to this: human beings are destructive, evil, and despite all programmes of enlightenment and education have not fundamentally changed. But where people are accused of their sinfulness in principle, grimly, sadly and zealously; where the church reserves to itself liberation from sin through confession, penance, and the eucharist as a means of power or – as in Protestant circles – a bad conscience drives people to good deeds and some kinds of activity, no liberating powers grow. Asserting in principle that we are sinful can really only stimulate a basically bad feeling which does not make people clear-sighted or wise or free. It inhibits energies and at most produces activities. It stimulates the 'body of service'.

The Swiss psychotherapist Annie Berner-Hürbin sees this as a psychological disaster: 'Church history is a telling example of the dangers of being imprisoned in the negative and the loss of numinous powers of life which runs parallel to this: whether there is still enough power in the material of the Christian tradition for it finally to allow or even encourage comprehensive subtle relationships or, if this is impossible, to give itself relevant help could be decisive for its survival – in whatever form' (Berner-Hürbin, 210f.).

In the Jesus movement she sees the development of an 'interpersonal, subtle eros' which is called agape (ibid., 171). But this 'movement arising from a comprehensive eros impulse' has increasingly 'developed into negative attitudes like guilt, sin, depreciation, xenophobia to the point of the measures of the Inquisition, the refusal of love, excommunication and finally a sado-masochistic structure'. However, eros is unthinkable without the body. The Christian tradition 'no longer provided any pattern of development of eros from the physical to the spiritual; rather, the body had to be killed as quickly as possible, since it was imprisoned in "sin". Christianity wanted as it were to make the jump to the highest illumination, but lost the intermediate stage and thus usually did not reach its goal . . .' (ibid., 179). Given the increase in the number of people leaving the church, this analysis should make us think.

The most striking example of sin as the ticket to Christianity is the traditional eucharist. In the Catholic rite, communion is introduced with 'I am not worthy that you should come under my roof', and the confession before communion in the Book of Common Prayer speaks of 'our manifold sins and wickedness which we from time to time most grievously have committed'. Many women, and men too, complain that both are humiliating, that they deprive one of courage and pleasure in taking part in this meal and experiencing it as a liberation. Sin as a commonplace, without grappling with current, personal sin today, turns much upside down. A grey tinge of death, farewell, sacrifice – images which do not uplift but oppress, arouse guilt feelings and belittle people – is for an increasing number of people connected with this most important ritual of Christianity.

Cosmetic changes like omitting the confession will not change the substance. A reorientation of Christianity must begin with a rediscovery of the body and its energies, for only in this way can the power issue from it to be 'salt' in present-day society. Just as the woman in the story with which I began draws living energy from the body of Jesus and can now go her way in wholeness, so with his body we could receive, taste, hand on whole life – life which is not simply a sacrifice, but dedication to a cause, the cause of righteousness. Here it would be possible to bring this earliest Christian meal to life again with all its delight in the senses and the communion and relationship experienced in it.

It is, for example, a farewell meal which stands for many of our farewells from which processes of maturing can develop, and which expresses the whole intensity of such togetherness.

It is a strengthening meal which gives physical and spiritual energy to follow one's way alone.

It is a commemorative meal of events in the life of a person who had a special radiance for others which can be experienced once again.

It can also be an ecological, cosmic meal in which we taste God and participate in God, who will not give up his/her endangered and holy creation, the earth.

There are many possibilities, but are they strong enough to combat the death-wish of ecclesiastical Christianity?

That Jesus sacrificed himself for human sin is a statement which is disputed even in theology. At least, it is incomprehensible to an increasing number of people who are rediscovering religious sources in the Sermon on the Mount and the Jesus movement. If we understand Jesus as the one who went before us in his life and death, whom we need not and cannot imitate, but whom we can follow because he was credible and passionate in his life and in his commitment, then the eucharist can again take on meaning as a meal of fellowship, remembrance, creation and the senses, and as a promise of our ultimate and final wholeness.

A Christianity in process of renewal in no way denies the negative aspects of life. But we must note the traps into which we fall. An order of confession in Baden reads, 'nothing good dwells in our flesh and blood . . .', and (addressed to God), 'I have loved myself more than you'. But here one may ask how anyone can love their not-being-good at all, what love is in that case, and whether such love of God is not macabre in the extreme.

The different ways in which 'sin' can be experienced is shown by a confession composed by Swedish women. Women in particular ask today: 'Aren't there sometimes other sins to confess than those that we've let ourselves be talked into?', and here suddenly the body, suspected as the suppressed and secret place of sin, becomes the focal point of our 'guilt'.

God,
I confess before you,
that I have had no faith in my own possibilities.
That in thought, word and deed I have shown contempt for
    myself and for my ability.
I have not loved myself as much as others,
neither my body nor my looks,
nor my talent nor my own way of being.
I have let others direct my life.
I have let myself be scorned and mistreated.
I have trusted the judgment of others more than my own,
and allowed people to be indifferent and malicious to me without
    objecting.

I confess
that I have not developed to the extent of all my capacities,

that I have been too lazy to fight for a just cause,
that I have wounded myself in order to avoid controversies.

I confess
that I have not dared to show how brave I am,
have not dared to be as brave as I really can be.

God, our Father and Creator,
Jesus, our Brother and Redeemer,
Spirit, our Mother and Comforter,
forgive my self-contempt,
raise me up,
give me faith in myself and love of myself (Lena Malmgren).

A similar confession for men and women from England, by Janet
Morley, says:

We confess our misuse of sexuality;
we have found pleasure in the degreading of others' bodies;
we have failed to respect and care for our own bodies;
We have chosen to condemn, rather than to delight in each
other . . .

Here religious interest is shifting to energies in people which have
not previously been tapped – above all in women.

A body-reformation of the church could change much and also
restore body to the many moralistic, abstract, laborious and strained
sermons. Here are some suggestions for the embodiment of
preaching:

1. No sermon should be without an urgent image or a central
story in which hearers can get involved.

2. Every biblical text can stimulate associations with symbols
which can be offered without suspicion of syncretism through fairy
tales and myths. Symbols reach depths in human beings which move
their bodies in a different way from purely rational discourse.

3. We need promises of salvation which do not derive from the
legal sphere but from physical bodily notions. There are many of
them in the Bible, and they remain unknown and unused only
because of our narrow theology of sin. In them people do not come
before a tribunal but into a communion with God which embraces

them totally. Instead of the constant talk about sin, forgiveness, justification, there should also be emphasis on being healed, becoming whole, mending the rents, binding up the wounds. The Hebrew word for save (*yasha*) basically means creating room, not being under compulsion.

4. Even a spoken word, even preaching, need not be a burden on the head and one-sidedly rational. Words can also change our bodies – biochemically or electro-chemically. It is not a matter of abolishing preaching and with it the culture of the word. The important thing is for language to open up space which does not limit us but which moves us, make us experience, have a breath of other things: 'You set my feet in a broad room' (Ps.31.9).

Stories of healing

In contrast to the church tradition, which was always tormented by the inadequacy of the body, the New Testament begins with a confession of God's good creation. We should turn to this tradition again and enliven the Christian community. It is said of Jesus, 'He has done all things well; he makes the deaf hear and the dumb speak' (Mark 7.37). Here is a reference back to the creation story in which God saw that everything was very good (Gen.1.31). With the coming of Jesus a new creation begins which is similarly good and beautiful. If we want to get out of our distorted and barren Christian thought-patterns, we can find a new orientation here for what is whole, holy and good for us. If we want to begin to trust our bodies and ourselves and to believe that they have capabilities, then we should read the stories of healing as our own healings.

Here, too, the male body alone is no longer the norm. Women and children are also healed. The disciplined, enslaved and oppressed bodies are healed. We read stories of the healing of many men, a number of women and some children. Old (e.g. Mark 1.30) and young are healed, and some who are already thought dead.

People are not just healed of physical defects. Blindness, which is at the head of the New Testament ailments, is not just blindness of the eyes. It affects the whole person, who can no longer cope alone. But it is at the same time also an inability to find one's own way of life. Those who are healed ultimately go their way independently, talk of what has happened to them, or, like Bartimaeus, follow Jesus on the way (Mark 10.46f.).

Deafness and dumbness are no longer simply an inability to hear and to speak. They are also the inability to take in something else and to find our own language. Words come bubbling out of those who are healed.

Lameness is not just arthritis, rheumatism or a disease of the muscles. It is also difficulty in being independent. Those who can move again are required to take up their beds, i.e. cope with themselves and their past.

Leprosy also means exclusion from society. Usually those who are healed are sent back into their families.

A father-son conflict seems to underlie epilepsy (Mark 9.14-27). Behind the possession of the daughter of the Syro-Phoenician woman lurks an unresolved mother-daughter bond (Matt.15.21-28; Mark 7.24-30). The parallels to the Greek saga of Demeter and Persephone are striking!

The New Testament knows two different forms of illness. First there is possession by an evil spirit which has robbed the person concerned of his or her self, or centre. Secondly, there are various illnesses which are really called 'weaknesses', in which the inner centre of a person's power has been disturbed (Seybold and Müller, 126ff.). Healing consists in people recovering of their own accord or having the living force which emanates from them strengthened. Someone who is constantly taken, carried, pushed around becomes independent and is not a convalescent who needs looking after again. Nor is such a person obliged to become a disciple. How they decide on their own careers is now up to them. We have both models: healing and discipleship. Or, healing and a highly obstinate manner which Jesus often did not like.

It is striking that women are not afflicted with the classic illnesses – blindness, deafness, dumbness, paralysis – which according to Old Testament prophecy the Messiah will heal (Matt.11.5; Isa.35.5,6; 61.1). It is simply said that women and men are possessed by a spirit; the healing itself is not depicted (Luke 8.2). Women appear with new ailments which have no male parallels: fever (of Peter's stepmother), bent backs, bleeding from the uterus, the apparent death of Jairus' daughter. In these illnesses it is not an external limb that is affected, but the whole person from the centre. And the healings have much more far-reaching consequences than simply the regeneration of an organ. It is not just that the mouth pours out words, the feet support again, the bed can be taken away. In any healing of a woman a greater social relationship is restored, one which was lost or perhaps was never there. The bent woman who is now set upright again is told that she too is a 'daughter of Abraham' – a break with the patriarchal spiritual heritage. The woman with a bleeding uterus is promised *shalom*-totality, an end to the religious and social exclusion caused by her bleedings. It is said of Peter's mother-in-law that after being healed she 'served', a special expression for the involvement of women in the Jesus movement, which has nothing to do with our feminine availability. It is work to restore righteousness, of the kind also attributed to Jesus (Mark 10.45).

Jairus' daughter can now finally grow up and cross the threshold of her twelfth year. The daughter of the Syro-Phoenician woman, whom we have only got to know from her mother's perspective, is healed – behind her mother's back.

I would like to see this as women with their enslaved bodies, which displayed damage that seemed impossible to heal (even the fever which sounds so harmless is a demonic illness according to the understanding of the time), becoming healthy and in so doing entering into a new social, family and religious relationship. They are put on an equal religious footing, freed from ancient blood tabus, taken into a new movement towards justice, freed from the cares of a mother and the fussing of parents. It seems to me that there is a particularly close connection between the illnesses of women depicted here and social liberation. In these stories, women even more markedly than men demonstrate the dawn of a new age after their psychosomatic healing.

Perhaps the liberation of the oppressed child's body is also already envisaged here. We have some stories which point to this. It is not clear how old the daughter of the Syro-Phoenician woman is, but the conflict seems to go back a long way, perhaps into her childhood. She is torn apart by an evil spirit. She has no centre for her self (Matt.15; Mark 7).

The epileptic child carried by his father and probably also spoon-fed is a child who later becomes terrifyingly independent (Mark 9).

Jairus' daughter is on the verge of becoming a woman and may not cross this threshhold. Father and mother stand in front of her with love and concern (Mark 5).

The stories about children do not show misery and neglect but more an excess of family feeling and maternal love. Just as Jesus wanted to go his own way at the early age of twelve, so these children seek their own life-style to the point of manifesting refusal through illness. 'Suffer the children to come to me and forbid them not' – this is not said by a Jesus who simply 'loves' little ones but by one who was himself a disobedient son rebelling against his mother. Jesus pressed the children to him, took them to his heart, and in so doing gave them the message that they should become fruitful and independent beings.

Lastly, let's look at the distinctive features of the healing of men. If we do, we find a regular pattern: men throw themselves to the ground and ask for mercy. They give up self-awareness, hardness and all false discipline. They are shaken to the core and feel thay they no longer have a chance. They are no heroes. They have defects which make them useless in society. They often call visibly and loudly for healing, something that among the women only the Syro-Phoenician woman does for her daughter. Then they in no way always draw the consequences of what has happened to them. Some react with a changed life; others are forgetful and indifferent.

Luke, who was very concerned that men and women in his church should be equal, and in so doing wanted to express the difference between them, has very aptly depicted two parallel healings on the sabbath. The woman has a bent back, and her whole being must be set upright (Chapter 13). The man has a paralysed right arm which makes him incapable of work and useless in society (Chapter 6). He can only work clumsily with his left hand. He is only half there. At first sight his sickness seems more harmless than that of the woman. But it affects him just as seriously as a man, because it affects his capacity to work and his self-esteem. His right hand is guided by the left half of his brain, and that is the logical, arguing, analytical part used above all by men. This seems to be destroyed, paralysed, so that the paralysed man does not do anything himself, does not even have himself brought by others, but merely comes, is simply there, and sits silently with his damage and despair. This does not seem to be a notable or a striking illness, but Jesus discovers it and discloses it; he sees the illness as life-threatening, one which will not tolerate any delay. Here someone is perishing, in silent suffering, passively, and is losing his social context. For that the sabbath must be broken. Here healing means reactivating the right hand so that the man can now live as a whole being, with his own activities and experiences, his understanding and feelings: 'And his hand was restored, as sound as the other' (Luke 6.10). A man is restored to himself.

Touching and being touched

We get a bit closer to the healing stories if we do not remain fixated on Jesus the miracle-worker but look more closely at the processes of becoming whole. Accustomed to start from the almighty word and its sole power, we have overlooked how important the touching of the sick is. Our senses, above all our tactile senses, have long been stifled in a verbal culture. We are reading the stories with new senses today and are touched by the skin contact that is reported on them. We can very rapidly translate the apparently magical element in these stories into our own present, if we are open to what touching means for our own modern existence. Touching grasps, stimulates, changes our bodies. Words, too, can have something of the same effect. But they can also resound ineffectively. One cannot miss a touch. The body notices being touched.

The medium of touching is the skin. Let's first turn to its significance and function, which is being rediscovered today, but which for more than two millennia was the same.

The skin is our largest but also our least known organ. It is one of the organs of the senses like the eyes, the ears and the nose. It thus belongs with the group of sense organs which develop smell, taste and feel; the other sense organs, eyes and ears, are more familiar to us, conveying experiences like seeing and hearing.

What makes the skin unique as compared with all other organs is that it is turned both outwards and inwards, so that it can communicate what is happening within us outwards and outside experiences inwards.

The skin covers the body, is about 1.6 square metres in area, makes up a sixth of our body weight and is divided into an epidermis (upper skin), dermis and subcutis. It protects the body against external stimuli, stores fluids, regulates warmth and exudes sweat and poisons. As it is the largest organ, its nerve centre is also represented most strongly in the brain. It has a great variety of functions, transmitting cold, warmth, stimuli causing pain, itching and tension, and general feelings of pressure and contact. No one can survive without it, whereas people can live without eyes and ears. Its psychological function is as comprehensive as its physiological significance, as we shall soon see.

However, the skin is mostly an unknown organ to us, the importance of which we overlook. It does not seem to be an active organ like the eye, the loss of which we immediately detect. We usually notice the reactions of the skin when they are unpleasant, when it gets red, goes pale, exudes sweat, produces goose-pimples, is diseased or broken. If we don't feel anything, it seems to us to be normal. However, to 'feel' this normality could help us to greater sensitivity to our body and our environment. The skin is also the organ which visibly gives away youth and age and – as youth has become a cult – can set off alarm signals in people. The first wrinkle can then be the way out! Its functions as a surface usually make the skin seem very superficial to us. But those who suffer from skin diseases, of the kind that the author John Updike keeps describing, have difficulties with their self-esteem. The colour of a person's skin is still taken as a signal for what is within. To be tanned seems to white people to be healthy and dynamic. Black and yellow skin has long discriminated against those who have it, and rethinking in this area is still far from complete.

Unlike ourselves, our language still contains deep-rooted experiences of what our skin means for us. 'Thin-skinned' indicates great sensitivity. 'Thick-skinned' points to the capacity to allow unpleasant things to bounce off. What gets 'under our skin' is something which obsesses us, and so on. So the skin comprises our own most personal realm, and is a protective covering for our intimate sphere.

The special thing about skin is its capacity for perception. Its sense of touch enables it to communicate with the world and again to feel the world. The significance of perception by touch is becoming increasingly clear today. Helen Keller, who was born blind and deaf, touched the world and in this way learned to communicate. What people normally communicate to the brain by eyes and ears can also be communicated to it by the skin's sense of touch. What we may not 'touch' we may later find difficult to 'understand'.

This capacity already begins in the embryo – long before ears and eyes form. The embryo communicates through the skin with its environment, the mother's body. At birth this primal state ends, and a far-reaching change takes place: the contractions of the womb stimulate the child's skin and prepare it for the new state of independence. In animals, the mother licks the newborn offspring to make this process possible. In human beings the process of change, without which a child would be incapable of life, takes place through suckling, stroking, lying on a parent's lap. For the unborn child, the skin was the organ of experience and learning, and this continues with the baby. What it learns through its skin – tenderness, indifference – shapes it. By contrast, what it sees and hears is almost secondary. At least, seeing and hearing are shaped by touching: 'The skin is the mother of senses and all the other senses derive from it.'

So the skin is the greatest organ of learning (Montagu, 211), even in a spiritual sense. Our language still betrays these connections. We are 'grasped' – we 'grasp'. We cannot grasp what does not grasp us. Or we 'grasp' only in a grasping, violent sense. Those who keep alive their bodies, their feelings, their skin as levels of communication will find it difficult to fall victim to an abstract 'grasping', but will constantly retain bodily thought.

In touching we experience the world and one another. In today's ecological ethics the skin and the sense of touch associated with it become unusually important. 'As I touch, so I am touched' (Meyer-Abich, 252). Experience of self and experience of nature coincide. The Western self bids farewell to manipulation and exposes itself to new experiences.

The most intense form of touch takes place in love. Unadorned skin also allows love to be experienced again. A French feminist has said: 'We have so often used cosmetics to please him that we have forgotten our skin. Outside our skins we remain far from ourselves. You and I far from one another.'

From the first to the last day, touching is experienced as assurance, confirmation of the self and healing. Physical healing can also take place in touching; for example, it can lower high blood pressure. An incubator can be dispensed with for babies if they are stroked and massaged several times a day.

However, there are also rituals of touching. The inferior in the hierarchy does not touch those above him. An American president cannot allow himself a familiar gesture to a queen. But it often happens that a boss puts a friendly hand on the shoulder of his employees.

In addition, different cultures have different types of touching: shaking hands, rubbing noses, kissing the hand in certain European circles, the socialist fraternal kiss, the 'holy kiss' in Paul which still existed in earliest Christianity.

However, many rituals involving the skin involve only males. Women are often excluded from them; as the lowly ones who are to be honoured they are made contact with (kissing of the hand) or are helplessly at the mercy of excessive skin contacts. They seldom initiate touching in public life.

Shaking hands with one of the 'great' people of the world gives many people a sense of deep confirmation. Something magic has gone from the great person to them. A small existence is confirmed and transformed by a great existence.

In the healing stories of the New Testament to which we now return there are different kinds of touching. There is the energetic *kratein*, grasping, rescuing from the anguish of death – an expression which is also used for saving an animal from a well. So Jesus grasps the hands of Peter's mother-in-law (Mark 1.31) and Jairus' daughter (Mark 5.41) and snatches them back from death. The same expression is also used for the dramatic rescue of the epileptic body (Mark 9.27). Women grasp the feet of the risen Jesus just as energetically, rescuing themselves, reassuring themselves; this gives them the assurance that he is alive and their existence is confirmed (Matt.28.9).

There is also the more official laying on of hands (*epitithenai*) by Jesus, with which the bent woman can set herself upright (Luke 13.13) and the blind man see again (Mark 8.23f.). Here the power of the healer goes over to the sick person in a special ritual. The power goes from the stronger to the weaker. Jesus himself is clearly seen as the source of power.

Another term for touching is *epilambanein*, seizing a person.

But the most interesting expression for touching is *haptein*, which simply means 'touch' and which occurs in several passages. It seems to be the democratic kind of skin contact, for Jesus touches lepers (Mark 1.41), children (Mark 10.3), disciples (Matt.17.7). And again – as was hardly the case with the other kinds of bodily contact – people touch him or his garment, which according to the traditional understanding is synonymous with his person (Matt.14.36; Mark 3.10; 6.56; Luke 6.19). Anyone who touches his garment is made whole. So the woman with an issue of blood also touches his garment and thus himself. The woman who was a sinner touches his feet (Luke 7.38). The risen Jesus says to Mary Magdalene that she should not touch him. So she probably ventured to touch him previously (John 20.17).

This *haptein* thus does not stand for any official rites, but for contact between people between whom energies can flow. These are loving, confirming contacts which raise people from the shadows in which they are. The lepers, the children, the women, the typically under-privileged get self-confirmation and experience acceptance in the loving consensus of humankind.

And Jesus in turn experiences love and recognition, confirmation of his way, when his head is anointed by the unknown woman in Bethany, when his feet are anointed by the prostitute. In his defence of the sinner he chides the Pharisee who is his host for the disembodied lovelessness of his hospitality. The Pharisee did not kiss Jesus on the mouth, anoint his head, wash his feet and dry him with his hair. The love of the great sinner lies in her body language.

The touching by Jesus and in earliest Christianity, in its manifold forms, later became consolidated in the tradition of the laying on of hands, in the gesture of blessing, in the anointing of the last rites. Here an element of skin contact remained in the church, but no life-giving mutual contact.

The apostolic succession which is communicated by the laying on of hands in an uninterrupted chain still contains the idea that body and skin contact are important confirmations of existence. But since they are communicated above all by a male elite to a male elite, they have already lost their earliest Christian charisma.

I touch and am touched. This knowledge creates a new community of those who had no confirmation for their existence, who as a result of sickness, their gender, or social contempt had found no acceptance and now themselves become those who give, challenge and confirm. In the church of the word, in a society full of phobias about touching, in which the deep significance of touching has been forgotten, we should look for forms of touching both old and new. To touch means to stimulate people in their whole existence, with their senses and their spirits, heal their brokenness and make them once again capable of contact, thought and experience: 'You will stretch out your hands and touch, and it will go well with you' (Carter Heyward, 185).

Resurrection and healing: the epileptic boy (Mark 9.14–27)

Here touching already creates new life: healing is resurrection. That is shown by an example from the New Testament:

And Jesus came to the disciples and saw a great crowd about them, and scribes arguing with them.

And immediately all the crowd, when they saw him, were greatly amazed, and ran up to him and greeted him.

And he asked them, 'What are you discussing with them?'

And one of the crowd answered: 'Teacher, I brought my son to you, for he has a dumb spirit; and whenever it seizes him, it dashes him down; and he foams and grinds his teeth and becomes rigid; and I asked your disciples to cast it out and they were not able.'

And he answered them, 'O faithless generation, how long am I to be with you? How long am I to bear with you? Bring him to me.'

And they brought the boy to him; and when the spirit saw him, immediately it convulsed the boy, and he fell on the ground and rolled about, foaming at the mouth.

And Jesus asked his father, 'How long has he had this?' And he said, 'From childhood. And it has often cast him into the fire and into the water, to destroy him; but if you can do anything, have pity on us and help us.' And Jesus said to him, 'If you can! All things are possible to him who believes.' Immediately the father of the child cried out and said, 'I believe; help my unbelief.'

And when Jesus saw that a crowd came running together, he

rebuked the unclean spirit, saying to it, 'You dumb and deaf spirit, I command you, come out of him, and never enter him again.'

And after crying out and convulsing him terribly, it came out, and the boy was like a corpse; so that most of them said, 'He is dead.'

But Jesus took him by the hand and lifted him up, and he arose.

This story tells us of the healing of a sick child, a severely ill, indeed incurably ill, child. The sickness is not identified with a sober word like blindness, deafness, dumbness. It is described in a dramatic way which is unusual for the Bible, with disturbing, inhuman images of violence. A small person is being torn apart in his body; he is not himself. Instead of speaking he foams at the mouth; instead of eating he gnashes his teeth. Instead of moving in a lively way he becomes rigid and lifeless. Instead of admiring the elements as a living force, he experiences them only as deadly dangers. Instead of enjoying life, life is driving him into suicidal situations.

The sickness which is depicted here seems to be a form of epilepsy. In addition, however, there is a second serious handicap. The boy cannot speak, perhaps cannot even hear; the evil spirit which torments him is described as being speechless and deaf. That means that the child is suffering a twofold burden. In epileptic victims there are regular phases of normal life. Here this normal life is impeded in pauses between the sickness by dumbness and deafness. The child cannot express anything of what he wants to say. Nothing of what he experiences emerges from him.

At first the main figure in the story is the father: he speaks, acts, tells of his helplesness and his disappointments. He has had a sick child since the first moment of this child's life. From the beginning his body has never been what any father expects of his son: a counterpart, someone who is like him, who will continue his life and inherit from him, and in whom he finds fulfilled everything that remained unfulfilled in him and for him. A son is his father's dream – above all in the patriarchal societies of that time, where daughters had to be married and paid for, and could never enter into their paternal heritage, outwardly or inwardly. The speechless son is a symbol of disappointment, of destroyed hope.

From the medical side it has even been said that a form of epilepsy can arise from such excessive expectations. The tenseness of the child can be the consequence of tense expectation. Healing takes place when the excessive pressure is removed, when the dominant partner withdraws his expectations and the counterpart is relieved of stress. Do we have such psychological illness here? Some of the later outbursts of the father suggest this.

At all events, we should remember that the illness described here is not simply psychological, and that the later healing is not just a miracle coming from outside and above. In its wisdom the Bible is deeply interested in the network of human relationships. Salvation and healing take place among us and through us. Here the father is deeply wounded, and he shows his wounds openly: he has left the protection of his home and made his child and his problem public. The expectation of healing, change, renewal, freedom which is that of the people in our story, is summed up for the father in the expectation: 'My son must be changed.'

What now happens is thus different from what we read in other stories of healing. There the complaint is immediately followed by comfort, the laying on of hands, the healing. Sometimes the healing is combined with words of clarification and interpretation. What happens here is disappointing. Jesus is reluctant, offended: 'O faithless generation, how long am I to be with you? How long am I to bear with you?'

Whom does Jesus mean here? The disciples who could not heal? The people? The father? I think that he means all those who do not grasp and bring to life this trust in the healing powers which are in this world and among human beings, those who do not trust like the disciples when they have the young man brought to them, and who have no trust in themselves and the power of God to change this world, those who have tried one saving doctrine and one guru after another and still have not been healed.

What now follows is a healing which is not a miracle – a process of human discovery which is never related again in this form. It is a way to power and trust, a way to faith – if we are ready to use a word which is so often misused and worn out in its original sense.

Jesus has the sick boy brought to him, but the result is a confrontation between the evil spirit who has taken possession of him and a power which poses a deadly threat to it. The child is the victim. He is seized, almost torn apart, and in a new attack falls to the ground, foaming at the mouth and with terrible spasms. This is a grim sight for those who expected a miracle, a grim experience of violence.

But there is something in the statement which makes us prick up our ears. The child has always been the object. His father spoke for him. *They* brought him to Jesus. The spirit tore him apart. But now we hear quite clearly that *he* fell to the ground. Now the child is suddenly no longer the object. He is himself. He is a tormented human being, but he is no longer just the plaything of the evil spirit, no longer just a something which has no capabilities, which has to be carried and looked after, for which someone speaks and acts, thinks and organizes. *He* fell to the ground.

This statement would not have made me think had it not occurred elsewhere in the story of Jesus. In Gethsemane Jesus fell to the ground in anguish and prayed God to make the cup pass from him. As there, so here the earth receives the pain, just as the drops of blood from the crucified Jesus are absorbed by the earth in Matthew, just as in the Apocalypse the earth absorbs the dragon's water and swallows up his wickedness, so that it can no longer harm the woman.

Our fear of magic has made us forget God's comforting companions: water, wind and earth emanate powers which help us to cope with life. But if we read the Bible, and above all the Gospel of Mark, the earth is an active, independent power, a good, divine power, *magna mater, mater terra*, mother earth, It makes the seed grow, just as in the creation stories it brings forth green things and plants. It quakes in anger at Jesus' death. It gives up the dead. It opens its mouth and swallows up evil. Here it catches the boy, in a hard but healing way. Here the process of healing begins. Here no solution either from above or from outside is yet visible. Here a human being falls to the ground, seems to collapse, and yet finally begin to live, for the earth with all its secret power swallows up the pain. In our burial liturgies we still have images of earth and resurrection: 'Dust thou art and to dust thou shalt return.' God will raise you up from the earth at the last day.

Like a good doctor or therapist, Jesus now begins to ask the father about the history of the boy's illness, and the whole misery of the child's environment is once again developed. The father, too, must once again go quite deeply into the reason for this sickness, this life-long, life-threatening sickness. He relates how the spirit has thrown the child into water and fire, i.e. first of all how the child has had to endure every conceivable danger and has emerged from this hurt and terrified. But in this description of the boy's illness, in the images of fire and water, he is already describing himself, his own being torn to and fro between the extremes: between love and rejection of the child, between loving care and hatred, between forgetfulness of self and love of self. In his explanation of the illness he declares himself, gives up something of himself. We can put it like this: 'Help me, I am just as much in need of help.' 'Have mercy on us. Help us.' That is what emerges. Now the story has suddenly turned around. We no longer have a healthy father who brings his sick child. We have two quite different sick people, both of whom need help. One of them is lying on the ground. The other is still standing. But he, too, begins to fall to the ground. Hidden, concealed, invisible things lie at the basis of our existence – drives, anxieties, longings, feelings – and the man is overwhelmed by them. They engulf him. Jesus does not put a stop to this terrible process, which is yet so important. He does not stretch out a helping hand. He does not provide any support. On the contrary, he only utters an enigmatic statement: 'All things are possible to him who believes.'

Is that support for someone who is sinking? Isn't it an impossible demand to fulfil? All things are possible – that arouses expectations of total power, of perfect fulfilment. But what is meant here by this 'all' is the opposite of perfection and total power. It is the wealth of God's life. It is the network in which we live, move and have our being. 'All' is not a word which is used lightly in the New Testament. It expresses something of the fullness of the presence of God which we can grasp, in which we can live and give life. It is the power which people seek in history so ardently, and which is there in all fullness for the one, for those, who no longer want to live half a life, in anxious expectation. So I would prefer to translate this sentence. 'Everything becomes fullness for the one who believes.' Anyone who believes is confident instead of waiting and projecting expectations on others, and such people will have everything fully. Faith does not mean climbing the peak of the possible, but allowing oneself to fall to the depths of existence and be grasped by the length and breadth of life.

Why did you come to me? That is what the man has to understand. In yourself, and everywhere, are healing powers for you and your child. You must grasp them. Then you can be healthy. Then your child can become healthy. Your son no longer needs to be the sole object of either your love or your anxiety. You yourself need no longer be fixated on your role as father – with all its pride and also with all its compulsions. You can be a human being who lives from fullness, who needs no longer fear fire or water, but can live out to the full fire and water, passion and flux, aggression and calmness.

Jesus leads people away from their expectations of him as healer and takes them back to themselves – to their power, their dynamics, their faith, their trust. He leads them away from obsessions, from expecting miracles of others, from outside, and allows them to discover the possibilities that they have.

The cry with which the man reacts is a death-cry, a death-cry of the dependent, possessed personality. The word used at this point is the same word as that used for the cry uttered by Jesus at his death. It expresses something which had been hidden under anxiety, rigidity and expectation, and which breaks out with elemental force. Perhaps the father could no longer cry, no longer show his feelings. Perhaps his expectations for the child were too rigid. Later his attitude to the sick child was too compulsive. The one who believes or, better, who finds his way to trust, in himself or herself, in others, in the presence of the power and love of God everywhere in the world, will find all things in full. Such a person experiences everything in wholeness, full of relationships. All things will happen to you in fullness if you trust.

Let's return once again to the child. We've left him lying on the ground, in helpless spasms and yet giving back his pain to the earth. The child who is now no longer just the object of his father's care, anxiety and love, the child that has been let go of. But where has he been let go to? What will become of him? The evil spirit is still at work. He is still possessed by it, the object of its annihilating power.

The conversation between Jesus and the father does not seem to have been noticed by the public. Now the people is there with its curiosity, with its expectations. Where and how does salvation come?

where and how does everything become different? Where and how are our hopes fulfilled?

In this public, political, scene, Jesus shows what God's power, used publicly, is capable of. He admonishes the deaf and dumb spirit to come out of the boy and never return to him again. This is not a silent procedure. The spirit first of all rebels with all its might, and once again threatens to tear the child's body apart before coming out. As the father cried out in fear of death, as Jesus cried out in the distress of death, so too the spirit now cries out before leaving its victim. God does not come with gentle, soft rustling. Where God comes, what has gone in must come out. Where God comes, what is destructive and opposes life in all its variety is annihilated.

Now the child lies as though dead. Freed from his tormenting spirit, but without a life of his own. The people can only feel that he is dead. A Good Friday lies over all of them, and the great expectations have died.

But now Jesus takes the child by the hand, with that grip with which he kept raising up the sick, through which health, life and confirmation of their being were restored to them. Then he raises the child up, as he has raised up other sick people. The word *egeirein* which is used here is the word used to describe God's action in raising Jesus from the dead. And in this cautious raising, arousing, resurrecting, the miracle now takes place. The child stands up. All by himself. Perhaps for the first time, at all events for the first time in our story. He was introduced as his own person when he fell to the ground full of pain. He is now independent a second time, when, carefully raised, he stands up independently, someone who is no longer spoon-fed and looked after, no longer the object of anxiety and excessive love. The word 'raise' used here is, as I said, the word used for the resurrection of Jesus. Resurrection is not a myth or a dogma of faith. It is always already present. Now the boy can be independent of his father. Now he is no longer speechless and deaf. He has become a person, with his own language, his own dignity, his own story.

Resurrection of the flesh

In its creed today the church confesses the resurrection of the dead. We should ask whether this hope is contained in Jesus' message of justice and the healing of our bodies or whether it is a reaction to the only thing that we know with certainty in our lives, that we have to die, and that our bodies will be buried in the earth, burned, scattered on the sea or to the four points of the compass. Over against this sole certainty stands the greatest uncertainty, anxiety about death. There is something destructive about anxiety. It can devour us. It has power to swallow up and kill. Anxiety threatens not only our soul and our spirit, but the whole of us, our bodies in which soul and spirit dwell. It penetrates all our organs, makes them 'narrow' and can cause *angina pectoris*. Anxiety can possess us; it can make us sweat and turn our stomach to water. And the final anxiety is anxiety about death.

Does the resurrection hope have a meaning which rids us of anxiety?

Anxiety arises in a transition from a familiar situation to an unfamiliar situation, from the well-known to the strange. Children are anxious about dark passages, dark cellars. Anxiety is always about something dark, rigid, impenetrable. Similarly, people who have precisely this incalculable, rigid, unrelated character can cause us anxiety. Not everyone, however, has the same anxiety in transitional situations. It can also be combined with curiosity. If I can take something of myself into new places, something stable, certain, that I feel cannot be taken from me, then the anxiety diminishes.

Many other experiences of anxiety precede this anxiety about death. Death is an enemy which we meet in different forms. 'We meet it,' the psychologist Dorothy Dinnerstein writes, 'during our long infancy, during that period of dependence on adult care the adult's grief is preceded and preformed by the infant's grief at its lost sense of oneness with the first parent . . . The later knowledge that we shall die resonates with the pain of our earliest discovery of help-lessness, vulnerability, and isolation: with terrified sorrow of the first, and worst, separation (121).

But at the same time the personality, the self, develops here, though the experiences of that self always remain stamped with this destruction of the uncomplicated identity with mother, body, and a closed and supportive, unquestioning feeling about the world. To become a self the body is sacrificed as a place of security and pleasure, a discord which only ends in death. It is a discord which puts the body in question and brings the body of the woman in particular, this first, only and important point of reference for the child, into disrepute. Where the body is still the place of sin and negation – as in some traditions which call themselves Christian, the anxiety must become even greater.

Against this anxiety people have developed visions, visions which help them to take something with them into the dark sphere that awaits them. Elisabeth Kübler-Ross noticed a shattering document of hope and resurrection in the children's section of Maidanek concentration camp: on the walls the children had scratched countless butterflies, symbols of new, free life, which – as from cocoons – would emerge from their dying bodies. There are very different visions, great hopes for a continuity, for a further life. Usually they are brought together under the term 'immortality'. But even this immortality is given up to changing currents of time. Let's look at some of them more closely.

In her therapeutic practice, Anne Wilson Schaef observes three wishes to perpeutate oneself: 'One must either have children, especially male descendants, to carry on the family name and the genealogy; or one must accumulate material goods; or one must produce eternal values – for example, masterpieces of literature and science.' She experiences these wishes among men but not among women: 'I have yet to come across a woman who is concerned about her immortality.' Women, too, need confirmation from their children, but without the high expectation that this will guarantee them a kind of immortality.

Less material, but more widespread, is the old idea of immortality according to which the soul parts company with the body, so that the mortal remains and the immortal soul separate. Here the soul is immortal because it is unborn. In its nature it remains untouched by birth and death, and is the side of human beings which is turned towards the everlasting divine. Here the divine is thought of in the most unearthly terms possible: immortal, eternal, immaterial. By contrast, the body is a material covering, subject to the laws of life, of being born and dying. However, human beings can already detach themselves from it by meditation on death and become aware of their own immortality in their souls. This happens by their becoming free from the sensual experiences communicated to them by their bodies, so that they now directly enter their own souls. In such inner recollection they can already anticipate death, but they have also already cast off their bodies themselves.

These and similar visions of souls are to be found in many religions and philosophies down to the present. They are attractive because they forget the unloved, sick and meaningless body and seem to legitimate flight from the everyday and the body.

But they also need to be contradicted, because they catapult God out of this earth and make the conflicts within us and outside us seem insoluble. They prevent us from seeking and finding solutions on this earth here and now.

The idea that the earth is the last and natural place in which our bodies rest and are born is again of increasing attraction today. Comforting pictures of the earth already occur in the Jewish-Christian tradition. They have simply been suppressed by abstract notions of the spirit. When the Jewish girl Janina David learns that her parents have perished in the concentration camps, the earth for her is the element which connects her with the dead and at the same time gives her new power to live.

> I turned and hid my face in the long grass. The earth spun at a terrifying speed, hurtling through the eternal night, and I clung to it with both hands, flattening myself against its unyielding surface. If only I could be in it too, like all those who were already safely dead and buried! How secure I would feel! But I was outside, the earth did not want me, and there was no way of reaching those who were inside. It was no use beating it with my fists and crying to be let in. I had to continue to live out my allotted span – alone.
>
> I closed my eyes, pressed my back into the earth and repeated aloud: 'My parents are dead. They died in concentration camps or, betrayed by their fellow citizens, on a street of the city. I shall never know how, or when, or exactly where that was and where they were buried. There will be no tomb sheltering their remains. The whole country is a grave, the whole earth a vast

grave and, somewhere, they are part of it. I can go away now, but as long as I can touch the earth I will be in touch with them.'

Through half-closed eyes the brilliant sky glittered. There was a shimmering pattern of leaves dancing against its hard blue background. I woke up after a long sleep in which the scent of apples and pears ripening in the sun had miraculously returned, and even now was filling the air around me. The earth was soft. I lay on my back, feeling the ground yielding under me, like a warm cradle. Grass was grew between my fingers and over my body; ants crawled on my legs. I watched them calmly, without a shiver of fear. They and I, all of us, belonged to the earth. She was the only indestructible fundamental basis of all life. She gave us life, and we shall all return to her one day. This was the sole certainty, the only consolation.

From the orchards, dreaming in the autumn sun, the warm wind brought a scent of ripening fruit. A scent of life returning life. A scent of peace' (David, 348f.).

But recollections of such comforting power in the earth have also remained alive in Christianity. On the tombstone of Gregory the Great from the seventh century there is still the inscription. 'Receive, o earth, what was taken from your body.' And a funeral liturgy used today still runs. 'From earth you were taken and to earth you shall return. From this earth Jesus Christ will raise you up on the last day.'

Here old knowledge about a power of earth similar to our bodies has been fused sympathetically with the Christian hope of resurrection. The Latin American liberation theologian, Walter Rauschenbach, can pray: 'Grant that our body may return in peace into the womb of the great mother who has nurtured us and that our spirit can then enjoy perfect life in you.'

Gaia, the old earth mother, again spreads out her arms to receive the bodies of her children, since Christian images of resurrection, now incomprehensible, have become too lifeless for them. There is no introduction of a nature myth and an anti-goddess here. Rather, existing biblical images are being taken up, according to which the earth of which human beings are made does not simply mean dust, dirt and transitoriness, but always also has within it something of the substance of hope, fertility and renewal. This earth into which the dead bodies are lowered reconciles us with mortality because it keeps something of immortality hidden in itself. From such earth by tradition the Redeemer can also come: the grain of rice, the root of Jesse or Christ from the earth, as Christoph Blumhardt and similarly later Teilhard de Chardin saw him.

The American feminist theologian Rosemary Ruether makes clear the significance of the earth as the matrix which transforms our individual being into new communities and relationships.

> To the extent to which we have transcended egoism for relation to community, we can also accept death as the final relinquishment of individuated ego into the great matrix of being.
>
> All the component parts of matter/energy that coalesced to make up our individuated self are not lost. Rather, they change their form and become food for new beings to arise from our bones. To bury ourselves in steel coffins, so that we cannot disintegrate into the earth, is to refuse to accept this process of entering back into the matrix of renewed life. Such a manner of burial represents a fundamental refusal to accept earth as our home and the plants and animals of earth as our kindred. In this way we also fail to recognize the redemptive nature of our own disintegration-reintegration back into the soil.
>
> But what of the meaning of our lives; what of the good to be remembered and the evil redressed? Is this merely the disintegration of centres of personality into an 'impersonal' matrix of the all? If the interiority of our organism is a personal centre, how much more so is the great organism of the universe itself? That great collective personhood is the Holy Being in which our achievements and failures are gathered up, assimilated into the fabric of being, and carried forward into new possibilities (Ruether, 257f.).

In the face of such views of earth, some Christian images of resurrection which seek to describe the leap beyond space and time but remain in the abstract begin to fade. The notions of the 'spiritual body' in Paul are an example of such a laborious construct. Since in later Christian thought biology was dismissed for the problems of death and gender, many fantasies of the new life after death came into the realm of personal, male, but otherwise incomprehensible creations. Anxiety found only a sphere of fantasy; the separation from which it had arisen had not been healed.

Resurrection is understood by socially committed Christians as rebellion – a concrete interpretation with which resurrection is taken up into life. But that is not enough.

If we want to make a new start in bringing the Christian potential of hope, the strange and revolutionary element in Christianity, to life, we must begin with violated bodies. In them we must find confidence for the present and hope for what comes later. The pattern of relationships of our bodies is the foundation 'for holy being' (as Ruether puts it).

If we transfer the notions about the 'beyond' to this world, the body extends, becomes transparent. It can be liberated from the narrow limits of its own skin and feel the pains of others. It becomes open to love and can emanate love. The question which pastors' wives once put to Karl Barth, 'Will we see our loved ones again?', gets the same answer here: 'Yes, but also the others.' Only it has other dimensions. Here loving already includes the others, the strangers. What we see again has a prelude in us.

Our bodies, gnawed with anxiety, can become more relaxed. Here already the message applies that those who think that eternal life can be got only by doing can go down to the waters of life. Images from nature like water and wind (= spirit) are not just fortuitously and in a spiritualized sense images for new life, which can already be experienced now through water and wind. In the water we can feel ourselves being borne up, with all our limbs, as a whole person. In the fresh wind we can breathe deeply and feel the healing of dividedness.

'Don't be anxious', 'Don't be afraid'. That is the message which stands at the beginning of the incarnation, God's becoming body, and it can also accompany us as we become human beings. It is also the message of the resurrection on Easter Day, the message of hope that all that is cannot be separated from the love of God, whether blade of grass, or human being, or animal.

Wind and water put us in the wider context of all creation. The resurrection of the flesh, i.e. of all life, as it is already prophesied in the Old Testament, was for a long time the centre of the Christian creed. It is already under way here, in our own lives, in keeping others alive and in cherishing flora and fauna. We have reduced this central statement of Christian hope to a personal notion: to the resurrection of the dead in which only human beings are important, quite apart from the world as a whole or nature.

Eternal life begins here in us with our bodies, which can encounter anxiety over separation. It is not a leap into another world, but the healing of our world. We can pass this healing on to the living and the dying, who need touch and company, whose sense of taste and hearing is intact far longer than we think and longs for healing life. Then the way into the dark can be trodden with less anxiety. What, if anything, comes after that we do not know. But we can remain open to new experiences. The mysteries of a beyond still remain closed to us, since Jesus did not speak of them, but only of life, of body and of the world.

I can still remember a film about a dying Danish woman: ill from cancer, emaciated, with a narrow face and big eyes she lay in the living room of her home, surrounded by her family and her life's work – handicapped Vietnamese children for whom she had built up a special organization, whom she had brought to Denmark and many of whom she herself had welcomed into her home. Her daughter had now taken over the organization, and her own and other children kept coming and going in the house. The woman was often in pain during the filming, but she could talk of her work, her children and her illness, and at the same time stroke her cat and her cancer. In her ear she had a big gold ring, so that the students in Aarhus, as she roguishly said, would have something to laugh at when they got her body for dissection.

Here the work of the body and being a body had fused and taken away the bitterness of dying. Here an individual life had been abruptly broken off, but it was a successful life which had been incoporated into a greater life that was being carried on, and in the face of that, anxiety about death could diminish.

III

Being Open to New Areas

It's difficult when you want to do something
and your body, or part of it, doesn't.

(*Linda Sanford and Mary Ellen Donovan*)

There is more reason in your body
than in your best wisdom

(*Friedrich Nietzsche*)

Women's bodies as vessels

In the clinic of Erlangen University in autumn 1992 lay a brain-dead young woman, the victim of an accident, whose body was to bear her baby. Her body had been made a system of uterine care which was kept going with every conceivable medical technique in order to keep the foetus alive and make birth possible. Finally nature ended the macabre game.

Many groups of the population, women above all, protested against this abuse of the woman as a whole person, against the misuse of the woman's body. *Evangelische Frauenarbeit* appropriately wrote: 'The mother has been degraded to a vessel and an instrument.'

The image of the vessel kept occurring in the discussions. And it is not just a change image, but reaches deep into our present cultural self-understanding of woman and man, of women's bodies and men's bodies. How can we deal with it today? What other images can we put in its place?

The body as a vessel is an old notion, but it has undergone two very different cultural interpretations. In a matriarchal context the great vessel produces its own seed. It is parthogenetic and uses the male only as an opener and to disseminate the seed. By contrast, in the later patriarchal understanding it is only the place through which this seed passes and in which it is nourished. This patriarchal interpretation stamps the present notion, which already occurs in Plato, in the apostle Paul, in Judaism, Christianity and Islam, and keeps recurring in different contexts down to modern times: art, philosophy, theology, medicine. The image of the woman's body as a useful vessel corresponded to current notions deriving from male practice and male science, and society reflects this image in art and culture.

In painting we often find pictures of a woman with a jar or some other vessel beside her, less a reference to her activity as a housewife than to her bodily nature. The saints' jars of unguents, above all that of Mary Magdalene, are also vessels which symbolize the body. For many women these are still attractive images of totality, closedness, integrity. But we should also note the usual androcentric interpretation: the vessel is something that has to be filled. It is nothing without content. And it must be preserved with its content. It offers itself most attractively for notions of sexuality as devised in male society by men.

For the author of I Peter the wife is the 'weaker vessel whom the husband should honour' (3.7). For Paul, the woman is a vessel which 'every man knows to hold in holiness and honour'. The 'vessel' is associated with ancient and late-Jewish notions of sexual possession of the woman. For the male, sexual intercourse is using a vessel or instrument, and Paul unconcernedly made use of this familiar image (I Thess.4.4), even when he was arguing that the woman should be treated gently in line with a patriarchalism of love.

There are also social roles which correspond to these notions of sexuality. The male is active, and the female is receptive or passive, waiting to be filled (fulfilled) as a vessel. Without him her vessel is empty – both sexually and socially. She remains related to him, open like her jar.

The amazing thing, though, is that women's bodies continued to be vessels although biology developed, and from the seventeenth century it was already known that there were sperm and ova, and in the eighteenth century there were theories of 'preformation', which saw the homunculus either in the sperm or in the ovum. Although Goethe was familiar with the natural sciences, he summed up this prevalent image of the woman in a sentence which has become classic: 'Women are silver shells in which we put golden apples' (Conversations with Eckermann).

It is even more amazing that in discussions about gene technology our highly developed medicine continues to hand on the age-old image of the woman's body as a vessel. The Swiss theologian Ina Praetorius has demonstrated that in *in vitro* fertilization women are described as tubes and ampoules. This is the same view as that already put forward by Aristotle in ancient Greece, that the woman provides a location and the material for the male seed which gives the form (Praetorius, 76). Aristotle says: 'In the seed lies the formative power, so the male gives form to the female matter. The male bears within himself the origin of the procreative movement, the female the origin of the matter. The effect of the seed is to continue the tendency of the body of the seed to develop by its own movement. Only through the sperm is the creative force and perceptive soul introduced into the material.'

In her critical investigation *Woman and Nature*, Susan Griffin provides a present-day parody of this male world, of how the man regards the woman and nature and makes use of it:

It is decided that matter is passive and inanimate, and that all motion originates from outside matter.
It is decided that the nature of woman is passive, that she is a vessel waiting to be filled.
It is decided that in birth the female provides the matter (the menstruum, the yolk) and that male provides the form which is immaterial and that out of this union is born the embryo (Griffin, 5, 8).

The woman as person and subject does not emerge. Erlangen is everywhere.

Nowadays we know that the male is not the only one active in the process of the union of sperm and ovum. The ovum detaches itself from the ovary, goes through the fallopian tubes and nests actively in the mucous membrane of the womb: all these are active, deliberate processes of movement, rooting and growth. But that is not all: 'It is the woman's secretions and her muscular contractions which make the course of the sperm possible' (Olbricht, 129). The man's activity may be more visible and more spectacular. The movement of the ovum is invisible, but deliberate and powerful. Both sperm and ovum are mobile or can be moved (the ovum by a cilium) in different ways, and only in this way can they fuse together.

The pattern of life and roles derived from an obsolete biology are no longer any use. Our rethinking must not only cover the social roles of women and men, but also embrace nature and the body if it is to do justice to women and men today. But how can women reappropriate their bodies without seeing them as constantly related to . . ., as coverings to be filled, as material?

The old images of the virgin with the pot of unguent, which once expressed a kind of bodily independence in matriarchal thought, later veiled this independence. The content was virtue: chastity as the price of integrity and wholeness. The hidden garden, the sealed source – biblical images (Song of Songs 4.12), which express the closed nature of the woman as her true bodily nature – belong to the mediaeval symbolism of the body. The foolish virgins sadly hold out their empty vessels to observers. Marina Warner, the English art historian, draws our attention to a foolish virgin painted by Martin Schongauer whose body has deep cuts in it and is open above her stomach like the shells of a mussel or the lips of a vulva. There was no forgiveness for this, even if the painter indicates another view here which does not condemn.

There was no alternative to a closed or an open vessel. Nowadays, women are looking for new patterns of life related to their bodies, between steadfastness, integrity, totality on the one hand, and openness, transparency, softness on the other. The most impressive artistic attempt at this has been made by the American artist Judy Chicago. At her 'The Dinner Party', a gigantic triangular table laid for thirty-nine historical women, famous ancestors like Hildegard of Bingen, Virginia Woolf, Artemisia Gentileschi and others, she has shaped every plate with mandala-like, exploding suns, butterfly pictures, as she calls them, all of which have vaginas. They are meant to be female butterflies, but at the same time they are shells, flowers, meat, game – everything possible simultaneously. For Judy Chicago, woman is no longer to be understood in terms of conception and preservation, but in the creative openness of her body: a body which opens as at every birth, which can make space for its fantasies and visions, its thoughts and programmes, with a freedom from anxiety;

which can develop its spirit, a spirit that is nourished by the body, the senses, experience, the unconscious.

I found something parallel to this revolutionary, other, woman's self-understanding in a story about Jesus and women: in the story of the Samaritan woman (John 4). A woman who wants to draw water from the well with her jar meets Jesus, and in conversation with this woman Jesus develops an unusual image of human beings. Stimulated by this situation of the woman and referring to old female symbols (well = *pege* = goddess of the spring), he speaks of human beings as a spring. 'The water that I give to men will become in them a spring of water welling up to eternal life.' The woman, source of life, independent, natural, creative and spiritual life!

And then as the story goes on we are told that the woman leaves her jar, the jar, the vessel, her symbol as a woman, and runs off to tell her fellow-countrymen what she has experienced. She leaves behind her old female symbol, the jar, the vessel, because she may be something different: a source from which ever new, independent and living things can proceed.

If we reflect how many images of the closed physical vessel of the woman are taken from the Bible, e.g. the *hortus conclusus*, the closed garden, the 'sealed spring', then the revolutionary character of this image produced by Jesus becomes particularly clear. For if we read the Bible closely, it is striking that already in the Old Testament love song, the Song of Songs from which these images derive, there are images of openness: a 'garden spring', a well of 'living water that comes from Lebanon', as the lover calls his beloved (Song of Songs 4.15). This seems to me to be the model for Jesus' image. Our prudish past read out of the Bible what it wanted to read. It overlooked the openness which it might not see. The sealed spring which becomes the flowing spring is an unmistakable image which depicts the independence of the woman: body, soul and spirit. Furthermore, it could stimulate everyone, men and women, to make their skins porous and their bodies open and experience them as a place of their own unmistakable life. Then the instrumentalization of the body could be retarded and people could again be seen in their totality.

We find an underlying image of the vessel once again in the Gospel of Thomas, a Gnostic Gospel from a later time:

Jesus said, 'The Kingdom of the Father is like a certain woman who was carrying a jar full of meal. While she was walking on a road, still some distance from home, the handle of the jar broke and the meal emptied out behind her on the road. She did not realize it; she had noticed no accident. When she reached her house, she set the jar down and found it empty' (97).

One can certainly interpret this story in different ways. I would like to interpret it like this: it is not the woman carefully looking after her vessel but the careless one who does not notice her 'female' misfortune, thus contributing to the extension of the kingdom of God, who is the focal point of the story. God comes without our doing; God comes in our failures. God comes by breaking the female vessel.

Thinking with the body

Unnoticed by some loud contemporary movements in recent decades, the body has emerged from the shadow of the head. This can be seen from simple testimonies by contemporary men and women. It is reflected in an ecological philosophy little noticed by the public. It is a topic of medicine which is thus differentiating itself from the dominant technological medicine. It has become the topic of women, who here find a distinctive approach to their life and thought. And it could help us all to extend our restricted perspectives. The reversal is striking: the head, which for centuries was the crown of human beings, is only a part of the person. The spirit, which apparently originated from this head and constantly wanted to form matter, has been removed from its sphere of work. What was regarded as animal, as dull, unconscious, material, merely bodily, sensual, is becoming the object of new reflection and at the same time is being grasped as the subject of such thought. But the revolutionary element is that we are losing the distance from the object which has been inculcated into us and suddenly seeing ourselves as part of this object, putting an end to any cool lack of involvement.

Many experiences have led to such a reversal: technology, which was to improve life and which turned against life; experiences of illness which have led to despair over chemistry; a socialism which left out the senses and aesthetics; and not least the disaster with the Chernobyl reactor, which with its apocalyptic consequences put in question the foundations of rational thought. This return to the body is making headlines in newspapers. It is a process which is being crystallized by very different people in very different spheres of life, which is uncomfortable because it affects the whole existence of those involved and because it is opposed to patterns of life which have been engraved on them. For me it culminates in the simple sentence 'thinking with the body'.

Christa Wolf says something similar in her introduction to Maxie Wander's collection *Good Morning, Beautiful.* She says that 'women must understand with their whole bodies' (Wander 1978, 15).

The context of this sentence is the experience of the lecturer Lena K. She writes: 'When one has understood that life means not only joy but also sorrow, despair, helplessness and anxiety, then one will simply come to accept everything. One will understand not only with the head but with one's whole body that one must soak up everything, so that our life juices do not dry out' (ibid., 34).

Christa Wolf comments on this statement: 'We should safeguard this discovery, still very vulnerable, very little established; perhaps it could at least contribute towards putting in question the merciless alien rationalism of such institutions as science and medicine' (ibid., 15).

What happened to Lena K as a result of her social experiences as a civil servant, art teacher, housewife, levels which she could not connect because they were so contradictory, and what Christa Wolf understood as criticism of rationalism, seem to others today to be the alarm signals of nature. Human beings are feeling in their own bodies what they have done to nature.

For the philosopher Gernot Böhme, the age of the Enlightenment has arrived at a critical point. In the age of the Enlightenment human beings understood themselves as rational beings, and defined their bodies from that perspective. The body was something external to them: for Descartes another substance, for Kant something animal which had to be overcome in the course of civilization, the bestiality which must always be controlled and silence by the educational programme of the Enlightenment. But this defamed body is at the same time an expression of nature. And since the issue today is the integration of the nature of which human beings are a part, it is also the integration of the body. For human beings, the body is the primary way of 'being in the world and the foundation of self-awareness in feeling oneself' (Böhme, 33). For Böhme, the key concept of this 'being in the world' is sensuality. Sensuality is bodily presence. And that means two things. The environment can be felt where we are, and at the same time we disseminate an atmosphere. Now these senses are the decisive factors for our grasping and understanding. Böhme locates these new insights in an ecological aesthetics, the theory of perception.

For others, the new embodiment has proved the foundation for another epistemology. Whereas hitherto the contrast between understanding and feeling was the foundation of any knowledge, positing the repudiation of feeling and sensing, now feeling, sensing, sensuality are the media of experience and knowledge. Embodiment can be understood as a 'basic epistemological concept' which escapes the separation of reality into subject and object, into analytical thought and the intuition of feeling. Everyone is part of the whole. We need a participatory consciousnesss, an attitude which participates in and identifies with the world. The body is the medium of experiencing the world. For a scientist research can then mean extending one's body to the point that it accepts the object – so that one enters right into it (Fox Keller, 116ff.).

Apparently unscientific concepts like love and eros are also described as 'bodily' methods of approaching the object of research. By contrast, militant, conquering, penetrating approaches show the old division of subject and object. The approach typified by Barbara McClintock, who won the Nobel prize for her genetic research and who died recently, has been investigated and described as a respectful and sympathetic approach (Fox Keller, 158ff.). Respectful, because respect for difference is a basic condition of our interest in others. Sympathetic, because this is the highest form of love, which allows intimacy without doing away with the otherness. The vocabulary with which McClintock describes her researches is that of affinity, empathy, attraction. The boundary between subject and object has been given up without endangering science, because for McClintock science does not rest on division but calls for attention.

Do women have special gifts at this point? The question arises since women in particular have made important contributions in this sphere. The context of their lives has probably reinforced in them notions of being bound up with nature and of participation in nature. Moreover researches into matriarchal culture have shown them the connection between a women's culture and linked thought which was later overlaid by the experiences of male thought – separation from all the processes in the origin of human life. In male culture women were always associated with sensuality, the body, empathy – niches which were allowed them but which today, in parallel to some male thinkers, they are filling with new meaning.

Among the philosophers of a new embodiment like Gernot Böhme and Hermann Schmitz, who take up the old body philosophers like Jakob Böhme and Paracelsus, Bulgakov and Soloviev, there is one woman, Annegret Stopczyk, who especially calls her philosophy a body philosophy. For her, body philosophy is 'the attempt to find a specifically feminine way of knowledge which goes beyond the masculine ways of reason without completely excluding them'.

For her, all knowledge is related to the body: male knowledge, too, comes from the male body. But such body thought is opposed by a whole spirit/reason tradition. The foundation of male socialization and experience is detachment from the body and its origin. The result is separation and separative thought instead of linkage. But feminine body thought is still in its infancy, since women have usually adapted the separative patterns and have not again become conscious of their own bodies; indeed they even fear this as biologism. For Stopczyk, giving birth is an act of knowledge, so far not perceived in Western thought, in which the formative spirit or the spirit coming from above was always the creative element. However, woman is 'not born free but born woman'. Death makes all people equal, but birth makes each person unique. Women have not yet reflected on this uniqueness of their birth, or they follow Simone de Beauvoir in seeing it as an obstacle rather than an opportunity.

For Stopczyk, the catalyst for this new thought was the accident to the Chernobyl reactor. As the mother of a five-year-old child she began to mistrust all appeals by the authorities, the reasonableness and certainty of statistics. The foundation of this thought in the rational tradition seemed to her to be idiotic. For her, Chernobyl was the consequence of a worship of reason hostile to the body and to life. At every birth women are fighting with death. But Chernobyl was the death with which mothers cannot fight. Nevertheless there were parallels here to the anxiety and agony and the new knowledge which emerges, that life has an absolute value. The act of giving birth as an act of knowledge! The birth of a female recognition to trust the body, the stomach, one's experiences. This is not meant to be another ideology, but to make it clear that no insight can by-pass the human body any longer. Wisdom, Sophia is called for instead of a reason that does not do justice to life.

Stopczyk finds the first beginnings of such body thought in early Greek thought. In so doing she is following Hermann Schmitz, the body philosopher, who has shown that the figures of Homer's *Iliad* understand themselves essentially in terms of the feelings of their own bodies. An experience without the body was quite inconceivable. *Phrenes*, the diaphragm, the centre of the person, was later translated 'understanding', but was originally an expression of bodily processes, stimuli, affections. The interplay of the members of the body, their composition, was what knew. In the philosopher Parmenides, too, body and knowing are still one, but later body and soul were seen separately and the soul was put above the body. Language also still betrays such original connections with the body, reality, finitude. We describe what is spiritual, transcendent and thus beyond our bodily experience with the syllable 'in': infinite, invisible, independent, immortal. In this way a spiritual world was set up which was neither visible nor dependent nor mortal nor finite, and everything that was visible, finite, mortal and dependent – as what is born of the body – came to be despised. But body philosophy is giving these dimensions of real life in particular a meaning which again impresses on us our that we are born of our mothers, that we are dependent, visible, finite and mortal. Our Western tradition of flight from our bodies has driven us into the arms of death. So in returning to the body we are returning to the roots of our existence.

But how can that happen? How is body philosophy practicable? According to Stopczyk, thinking with our bodies would mean letting spontaneous influences which come to us from outside as feelings flow into our knowledge. Learning to think would simply be becoming sensitive to oneself, experiencing one's own bodily constitution more consciously, instead of overcoming it. In this way the learned concepts which haunt our heads and which we network like information would lose weight.

The question for this urgent scheme of the return to embodiment and finitude and thus life still remains whether women and men each have their own ways of thinking and living with their bodies. As we have seen, biological components and social experiences still drive the boy, the man, to the flight that Stopczyk attacks. Will men become mere inauthentic appendages to a culture of mothers? What could they themselves contribute with their bodily experiences of separation and pain? For Stopczyk it remains important to remind men of their intuitive gifts of knowledge, their suppressed feelings which they are not allowed to recognize. But what contribution they can make with their own bodies still remains open.

Like Stopczyk, the feminist theologian Naomi Goldenberg sees that feminine Western thought will be more bodily and more contextual as a result of women: 'The contribution of women represents the guaranteeing of the physical conditioning of all thought and every creation' (Goldenberg, 185). For her, women and matter are basically the origin of all our reflection, but both have been suppressed in our spiritual traditions. For Goldenberg, the goddess is the symbol of a new relatedness to women and matter. When theology returns to thealogy, the metaphysical returns to the physical.

Do we need the goddess for body thought? In what has been said so far we have looked closely into the relationship of Christianity to woman, body, matter, and here opened up sources for a new bodily existence. The Christian tradition which is rooted in the Jewish, total, thought of the Old Testament offers enough points of contact. The ideas which for many people so far have been improper,

– that God made himself body;
– that the spirit will become visible in the body;
– that God's energies cover the whole universe like a body,

are images which are alive in Christianity, but which our narrow and anxious churches trample on, instead of entering with them into a great free space of life and thought. It is clear that more women are needed here, above all women who think and live independently. If according to ancient tradition the church calls itself the 'body of Christ', it needs liberated bodies to deserve this name. The flight of many women to the goddess remains explicable, but it is not necessary.

One's own person

Hegel's notion of thought, which by-passes hearing and seeing, stands in abrupt contrast to thinking with the body. Hearing and seeing are the best-known perceptions with the senses, and ears and eyes are the sense organs responsible for them. Where they are deliberately excluded, thought has cut itself off from the body; it is robbed of the senses, and is therefore senseless in every meaning of the word. We must ask whether scepticism about the world and nihilism do not also have their cause in the split of the senses from our thinking.

Our senses are antennae of the body. They communicate to us processes in the outside world and conditions in our own bodies. They allow us to take a direct part in nature, and they express the pain, pleasure and pressure that our bodies feel. So the senses have a fascinating twofold significance. They allow us to experience that our bodies are not closed off, but have life in them which is lived outwardly and enlivened from outside. Through our senses our bodies are a unique communication between the self and the world, between our limited and often restricted space and nature and society, which give us a great deal of space. When we turn to the senses, once again we open up new spheres in which we may be as our bodies and with our bodies. These are spheres which are time and again barred to us; we must now open them to experience what we have lost.

Nowadays we make a distinction between the remote senses, eyes and ears, and the near senses which were originally much more significant: smell, taste, feeling, communicated through nose, mouth and skin. But the senses disappear, as was shown by the impressive investigation by Kamer and Wulf of ten years ago, which asked whether society too is not tottering and falling, like any individual whose senses disappear and who loses ground beneath the feet. But does the quest for the significance of the individual senses already perhaps show traces of a new sensuality?

First let's look at the individual senses and sense organs. The eye proves to be an organ on which excessive demands are made by modern society, in which for example traffic and television demand their due. Computers for adults and computer games for children burden our eyes. We have to learn to observe keenly in order to keep up with present-day life, and in turn we are sharply observed. The traffic camera watches us without our noticing. X-rays and computers scan our insides down to the last cranny. The eyes of secret police have watched millions of people. The eye of the big brother has sought to realize dreams of omnipotence, just as in former times the all-seeing eye of God was feared. From ancient times, many ideas of knowledge have been connected with images of seeing. Seeing is the sense of knowledge. Those who have not seen through something have not learned anything.

But all these visual images are remarkably disembodied. The machine eyes have no bodies and do not perceive us as whole people, but only our defects and our misdemeanours. Contemplation is forgotten in our culture of the eyes, which has also already been described as phallic. Contemplation does not isolate the eyes so that they become penetrating guardians of order, or analysts. Contemplation lets the eyes be involved in nature so that we can see ourselves illuminated by the light of nature. Goethe expressed this poetically: 'Were the eye not sunny, how could it look on the sun?'

But contemplation at least has a niche in our culture. Not Goethe's view of contemplative thought, but rather the wish for 'control of the gaze and disciplining of the body have become socially relevant' (Kamper and Wulf, 1984, 30) and have instrumentalized our eyes.

If the eyes suffer from excessive activity, the ears suffer from the need to accept passively a background of noise. Traffic noise, disco music, musak in shops and other public places prevent real hearing and impose on us a permanent burden of compulsory hearing. But hearing – even if it seems passive – can be an extremely active stimulus to our body which has a healing effect, as music therapies show. 'Listening to' is an art of hearing which combines activity and passiveness and which we are increasingly losing. It has necessarily to become a profession in which advisers, group leaders, therapists are picking up the elements of an art which has been lost in the private sphere. Here 'listening to' with interest is an unsuspected possibility of bringing people together in movement and counter-movement, exposing oneself to the vibrations which are experienced in the body.

We are least aware of the tactile senses, smell, taste, feeling, and their significance vanishes most rapidly in public. Like the remote senses, at first they suffer grave distortions in society. As we have already seen, feeling and being touched have become a painful matter. Taste has been privatized, and smell is below the belt for society. The perception of these senses cannot be objectified. Smelling, tasting, feeling, remain in the sphere of intuition and accordingly are regarded as subjective, unprovable and deceptive. The senses can certainly be deceived. But not to want to have perceptive tactile senses, to forget nose, mouth and skin as active and passive sense organs with a vital function for our life and experience, thought and action, is to rob our bodies of their own capacity for expression.

In the meantime, the sense organs of skin and mouth have been rediscovered by psychoanalysis: the skin as the largest organ which comes at the beginning of learning and loving; the mouth as an oral sphere in which something of our incarnation takes place. The nose is still an outsider: for a long time it was regarded as a sexual symbol corresponding to the penis. For Kant the sense that goes with it, smell, was the most ungrateful and most dispensable, although he had to acknowledge its warning function. One could and can least escape the emanations of society. Above all the negative ones are registered, and they in particular demonstrate bodily processes: corruption, poverty, sickness, signs of dying and death. Nothing documents human transitoriness more strongly than the nose. As compensation for such unlovely mortality, the mediaeval saints and their dead bodies were said to give off a pleasant smell, thus expressing a sensual hope of resurrection.

However, taste and smell are miles from their origins. We overemphasize unpleasant smells. We taste and smell more art than nature, and we taste and smell more of cosmetics than of the body. Here original taste and natural smells are now again being valued more highly: strawberries ripened in the sun, potatoes grown the old way, the smell of fresh wood, are again precious and rare experiences.

With smell and taste we perceive life as renewal and death, as vitality and decay. We are stimulated but also repelled, and through our bodies we can experience reality and ourselves as part of this reality.

In addition women have their own experiences and their own history of the senses. Traditionally woman is fixated on the senses, while man is given the apparent opposite to the senses, reason. Thus sensuality and understanding are divided so that they are gender-specific. A saying of Muhammad's has been handed down: 'Three things I love most in the world: women, good smells, and my solace in prayer.' Women have been revered and honoured as objects of sensuality, and at the same time that means that their capacity for understanding has been underestimated. The expression of the senses, the representation of them in the family or even in public, has long been regarded as their special task. But this sense has long been without relevance in society.

Here something has been inculcated which is presumably not rooted in every woman. Many women today recall that their 'own sense' had to be tamed or driven out. [There is a word-play here in German which is impossible to render in English: 'Eigensinn' conventionally means obstinacy, wilfulness.] This was regarded as being uncontrollable, contrary, irrational – quite different from having one's 'own power' ['eigenmächtig', another impossible word-play, conventionally meaning 'authoritarian'], which is still something of a compliment. Wanting to be their own persons instead of adapting – that was the problem posed by daughters to many parents, who sought to prepare them to be pliant wives. Wanting to be one's own person – that was ugly and dangerous. In their childhood memories women often relate how unnerved parents wanted to cure their small daughters of this desire for independence with brutal methods.

Where it was broken, there remained a broken sensuality which not longer comprehended the whole person with intuition and understanding and became 'woman-specific'. It was said to create a sense of beauty, harmony, warmth and balance, yet it simply reflected the splitting of society into a private and a public sphere.

Let's go on to consider individual sense organs, how they have been deformed, and the possibilities of developing them.

Women have long used their ears to listen to others, to those standing over them, to those who apparently knew better. And hearing led to obedience, this absurd reaction of the underling which again made women dependent children. The one who only hears, belongs, obeys, does not mature and become a person. Perhaps it is also because their ears have never been used rightly and independently that women like listening to rumours, making inferences, spreading secrets, but neglect the significance of total hearing. We should use our ears to listen to ourselves and perceive our voices which have so long gone unheard. When we learn to listen to our inner voices, our senses open up. Our sense of person grows again. Our perspectives change, perhaps making us first lonely and uncertain, but ultimately content with ourselves. Those who hear barely perceptible voices also become open to soft and suffering voices.

Women have long used their eyes to look away from themselves. That is what has been preached to them, and that is how they have seen their function of neighbourly and motherly love. The perversion of women's eyes is the evil eye, the feared, bewitching look of those who have no value of their own, who are compelled to look away from themselves and in so doing turn to hatred against others. It is difficult to see ourselves, for perhaps this confronts us with someone whom we did not know before. Seeing oneself brings anxiety, but it also brings the freedom to look at oneself unsparingly and without suppressing anything, to see oneself as unique. Those who have learned to see themselves develop an extended, generous, understanding eye for others.

For a long time we have marketed our skins, and with them our feelings. We have long been in the habit of developing feelings for others, but our own feelings, our well-being, were not allowed to be so important. But how can we develop feelings for others if we do not feel ourselves? How can we develop a sense of others if we have had to put a carapace round ourselves? Today's managerial training is aimed at developing an insensitive elephant's hide, insensitive to outside attack but also insensitive to others.

If our bodies awaken from the passivity attributed to them, our senses will again become our own. Just as waking up is not a transition to mere activity and domination, so too the awakening of our sense of self is defined by its receptive activity or active receptiveness, which gives birth, participates, allows to grow, shares, and represents the opposite relationship to the world from that of ruling and manipulating. The senses which we have learned to consider individually can then no longer be isolated. They combine and create new modes of understanding. They bring us back to our bodies and change our starting-points and ourselves. For example, the French writer and educator Fénelon remarks, 'When you are perceptibly touched, the scales wil fall from your eyes and with the penetrating eyes of love you will recognize what your other eyes will never see.'

Nellie Morton, the pioneer American feminist, has emphasized the vital importance of these sense organs for a new way of seeing, living and understanding: 'We learn to heed with the whole body, to hear with the eye, to see with the ear, and to speak with the hearing' (Moltmann-Wendel, 1983, 209). This revolution of the senses results, 'not in words resounding but in the word, breath and language of creation being heard'. What women today describe as 'wholeness', what expresses their vision of a successful life, is shown not least in this maelstrom of the senses which traditionally encounter us so separately. In the interconnected mobilization of them the body becomes a living experience and perceives others.

In what used to be East Germany, obdurate and utterly rational-ized, Maxie Wander, ill from cancer, sought this mode of experiencing with the senses. Right after the death of her daughter in an accident she began to heal herself by conscious sense-experiences. She wrote to a friend:

> I have devised an exercise for reviving my dead senses. To catch the nature and colour of every day with words, signs, signals. Like fishing lines . . . Today my day smelt of sunny fields, the breeze in the treetops, a millstream, forget-me-nots, Dani's bottom. Or the day begins with morning coffee, summer clouds, jays and saplings. Sounds in the wind, murmuring, splashing like water. Nothing. Everything . . .
> The next day in the Nikolai church in Geithain, Saxony. Looking down from the gallery at the high nave, dark blue with

brown pillars, brown like milky coffee, like a gypsy's legs. And sunlight streaming diagonally from coloured windows. A young man comes in, sits at the organ. His large, vital skull bent forward, intent, short-sighted. The thunderous sound of Bach. Old women in front of the pulpit, putting the flowers and fruit from the harvest festival in baskets and gossiping. A mild, brown noon, young for eyes and ears, old only for the nose; the old walls smell of dust (Wander, 1980, 126).

In her illness Maxie Wander began to ask questions. Where is life? Where is its middle and its beginning? And she began again tenaciously ('I cannot yet name it') to include the senses: 'One has to get wise to life and discover what it really wants; one must open one's eyes and nose and put one's ear to the trees as if to a mother's body' (ibid., 179). From these senses comes the certainty that nothing cannot be healed. What became important for her was to 'listen closely' where she detected that the life-force was disappearing, to 'breathe on it with our breath'. She asks what magic gives us such power and even ventures to resort to religion. For Wander it becomes important that we grasp more with our senses than ourselves and our fellow human beings. By reflecting on the senses she draws attention to the cosmic dimension of the existence in which we are bound up.

She did not as yet have something that is widespread today – knowledge of the life force, Chi, which, if we open ourselves to it, makes us transparent and, if we do not prevent it, joins us to the breath of creation. Where a split, an isolation, a separation develops, this life-force cannot flow, and that leads to destruction and sickness. East Asian and psychological insights can now help us to experience the meaning and sense of our lives better. The revived sense of one's own person opens up new broad ways through which one can learn to live more intensively. But that takes time. It takes practice and cannot be achieved in a moment, like much that we want to attain. The Russian writer Marina Zwetajewa wrote in her diary: 'For feelings in particular one needs time, not for ideas. Ideas are like lightning; feeling is a ray from a very far distant star. For feeling one needs leisure; it cannot live with anxiety' (Belkina, 94). Opening up the senses takes time, but at any time it can make us timelessly happy.

With our senses we can also experience another dimension of God. Not the God whom many people have learned in Christianity, the judge, master, ruler, the God from whom we remain eternally distant, but the God who is in all things. By again feeling the breath of creation with our many senses, we find that this God again comes near to us in this breath of creation. For in this God – as Paul says – 'we live and move and have our being' (Acts 17.28).

'The senses are nearer to God than ideas' says meditation culture. I believe that we cannot separate thinking of God and grasping God with the senses. In beginning to think with the body, to live with the senses, we can also attempt to think in a believing way with the senses. The rational consciousness which is developed in us and which runs contrary to this attempt could open up and allow another wisdom. In the end there is no barrier between sense and thought, any more than there is between faith and life. Many women can only engage in spirituality and politics – spheres which today are going in different directions – both together. We can again combine in ourselves what was once one. The dualisms which are created in us can be dissolved. What has proved in modern life to be apparently reasonable, logical separation could prove to be schizophrenia as our lives are emptied of meaning.

To believe with all the senses does not mean going off into a world alien to theology. It means engaging in a theology and again making the sensuality hidden in it capable of being seen, heard, touched. It means entering into a world which we can awaken as God's constant energy through our senses.

Bodies – spaces

The situation is always the same: it can be a prizegiving, an election meeting or a formal reunion – a man stands up to speak. He goes up to the lectern, buttons his jacket and adopts a posture. Sometimes he also straightens his tie and coughs. Thus composed, he communicates to the assembly that feelings and little untidinesses have been settled. He is concentrated. He is *he*.

Women in similar situations act differently. If they wear the feminine equivalent to the suit, it has been buttoned beforehand, or it is open and remains open. They almost never have a collar and tie as a help to concentration, so these cannot give any help. Women's clothes and body language have yet to find any special expression for such situations.

There are already very clear, different body languages for men and women in other everyday situations. Research and pictures show how differently women and men sit, stand, lie and walk. In a New York subway train Nancy Henley noticed that men lounge, put their arms on both rests, cross their legs by supporting one foot on the opposite knee. Their bodies expand and they dominate the space.

Women behave differently; they want to shrink. When they cross their legs they keep them close together. Their elbows are pressed closely to their bodies. They try not to touch anyone. They don't expand, but reduce further the space they have.

Our body is a space and it needs space. But this is dependent on gender, weight and how we feel about ourselves. Bodies can inflate themselves and extend; they can also contract and shrink. They can fill a space or leave it unfilled. We have different gender-specific body attitudes which express our lack of freedom.

But we all have spaces within us which we do not fill, which we overlook or block. Spaces for play, intermediate spaces which we should keep open, and which make our bodies with their organs, their limbs, their hardly noticed cavities, even more intelligent and mysterious to us. We have unused free spaces which we fill with our breath and our spirit and through which we can give expression to our vision of a whole life.

But in the end I want once again to connect our reflections on the body with the social phenomenon of space: where we reflect on bodies, we must also reflect on the public spaces that bodies need.

So our bodies claim a space, but they also need space to develop. Where someone occupies space at the expense of another a hierarchy arises, a gradation of power which curtails living-space and thus life.

The anthropologist F. J. J. Buytendijk described the male and female spaces of the bourgeois world of the 1950s and at the same time provided a classic model of an era which, while passing away, is still present. Many people still have these ideas. So we should note their significance for our self-understanding.

According to Buytendijk, the bodily nature of the woman is

expressed in face, figure, attitude and voice. Her 'inner space' appears outwardly. Buytendijk wanted to counter the disembodiment advocated by de Beauvoir, who experienced woman's body as her alienation, and understand the body again as the place in which we are in the world. Existence is always 'being a body in the world'. But here Buytendijk saw decisive contrasts between women and men, which also emerge biologically in the first period of life: the boy has a firmer build which is experienced as greater independence and leads him to develop an 'expansive aggressive dynamism' with which he encounters a world of resistances (Buytendijk, 245). In his grasp of the world his orientation is intentional. He is the later *homo faber*, who regards the world as material, and sees the purpose of his work as shaping this matter.

Buytendijk contrasts this expansive-aggressive male dynamic with the female adaptive dynamic (ibid., 251) which the girl develops. This is a way of moving which corresponds to the weaker build of her body, which adapts and is experienced in what it encounters not as resistance but as quality, form and self-worth. Instead of being war-games, which are what the coming 'workers' play, girl's games are skipping, doll's houses and ball games. At a very early stage they represent the later woman's world of caring and loving, which is not aimed at a goal, but whose highest culture is receptivity. What is biologically appropriate is reinforced by education.

However, Buytendijk already arrives at the conciliatory conclusion that in the future practical life will also mix the two different types of dynamic: care could also become a quality of life for the 'workers', and intentionality and understanding could transform an all too maternal magical women's culture. Nevertheless, the cultural and anthropological values which Buytendijk derived from the body in describing the feminine inner space and the male grip on outside space have once again conjured up the old gender stereotypes in which the woman does not have an active and influential place in society.

How do the spaces for women and men look today? Forty years later, this 'inner space' has again been researched, but without de Beauvoir's existentialist antipathy, which wanted to get rid of the body as an alien body on the way to being human, and without the romantic solemnity of Buytendijk, who summed up all this world's longings in his description of woman's space. In practice and theory woman has again approached the body and here has come upon old patterns and new divisions (Rose, 113ff.). It is again observed in researches how girls prefer limited space. Their games are skipping, rubber ropes and so on, for which they need only limited space: a courtyard or playground in the immediate vicinity of their homes. By contrast boys use nature quite differently as play space, with mountain bikes, skateboards and so on. Female inner space apparently requires less outer space. The outside space to be conquered requires other means for its conquest.

Investigations into gender-specific behaviour in sport show quite clearly that in recent decades women have also become involved in male sports like football; that sport and the culture of movement are taking on increasing significance for women, and as a result are opening up new spaces for them. But at the same time it is also becoming evident that the old inner space has really hardly been left behind: gymnastics and dance as a female culture of movement are exploding in great variety of forms. They are the domains of women's sport in which women have always been leaders since the beginnings of gymnastics and rhythmic movement. Ballet is and remains the dream of many girls. So again we should note the adaptive female dynamic as compared with the expanding male dynamic. Female charm and male aggression have not yet mixed convincingly in these spheres.

Some women note sceptically how the rediscovered sexual, aesthetic, sensual and medical body is reducing bodily dimensions to a minimum and blunting them socially. The public sphere is not yet full of women, is not yet the natural place for 'pleasurable experience of the body' (Rose, 118).

It is striking today how women want to preserve their bodies intact with these preferred kinds of sport. They avoid exposing themselves to the injuries which are readily associated with aggressive types of sport. Women are also less involved in accidents as children and later as adults – a positive sign of their insight into dangers, but also a sign of inhibitions about taking risks. Boys have more experience of the power and limitations of their bodies. Girls seem to avoid both these as far as possible. However, experiences

of violence in the home and on the streets are leading many women
to take up various forms of self-defence.

Perhaps this is leading to a new chance of experiencing one's own
body not only in its adaptive but also in its expanding and aggressive
dynamic. The hitherto deficient development of the body can be
pursued into the spiritual sphere, indeed it reflects this sphere:
where no risks are taken with the body, it will also be difficult for the
soul to develop a life of its own, and spiritual narrowness and
adaptation and a constricted inner space will shape thoughts.
Perhaps the notion of the extension of the body can be developed
further – beyond 'adaptive' and 'aggressive'. This would entail care
of oneself without limiting oneself.

We still lack such visions and also such encouragements. The
female body is still more the aesthetic, medical, sensual and sexual
body, which really only reflects its inner space and does not become a
public force. And similarly, the male body, brought up and designed
for aggression and expansion, which inflates itself, makes itself fast
and has great difficulty in sharing public space with others, has
hardly been worth any social interest. Despite many years of renewal
in thought, the terrains of women and men seem as divided as ever.
The question may arise whether terrains can be divided anyway, and
whether it is not here – as in the animal kingdom – that the harshest
defensive battles will take place, whether it would not be more
tolerable for the peace of society if the old rules were observed.

I have hopes for a new division and also for a political change
because of the experience that in the face of rising violence in society
women are being compelled to learn self-defence and also new
aggression to protect themselves. Sorry as the phenomenon of
violence is, it could be a helpful contribution towards a necessary
expansion of bodily aesthetics.

Another hopeful sign relates to the male body, the aggressive
potency of which is also connected with the repression of all
embodiment. The view of the psychologist Dorothy Dinnerstein is
that the male body which, despite the degree to which it is being put
in question at present, is so dominant and occupies so much space,
could have a hopeful future if it were as intensively involved as
women in the 'intensely carnal life of infants and small children'
(Dinnerstein, 150). Men need continually to learn anew the funda-

mental experience of the dyad, the dialogue, which stands at the beginning of life and which we are always losing. Then 'the reality of the male body as a source of new creatures is bound to become substantial for us at an earlier age than it does now, and to remain emotionally more salient forever after'. For Dinnerstein, this re-evaluation of the male body depends on the woman's body in its totality, with all its phenomena including birth, being no longer repulsive. If fatherhood and motherhood both mean early physical intimacy, according to Dinnerstein, the power of the man to procreate will appear as marvellous in its way as the power of the women. The fertile fluid that he produces is as powerful and at the same time as vulnerable as that part of her into which he pours himself. Together, both could protect the vulnerable element in themselves without being ashamed, without seeming contemptuous or superior. And he too could deal more carefully and protectively with himself and others, and change his claims to space (Dinnerstein, 151).

Finally, we could use the experience learned from the mother-child relationship of how to deal wisely with possible clashes of interest, or body space, to avoid cock-fights: children occupy a good deal of their mothers' body space. They make great demands on self-control, privacy and health. In turn, mothers can later have their revenge by forcing their way into the already independent lives of their children, a continuation of their ever-unsuccesful capacity to make their own space. Experience shows that it is difficult to separate interlocking spheres of life but that it is also possible to reshape independent spheres. It is a reciprocal process, involving pain and renunciation but also freedom and curiosity. This example could make it clear that we can never carefully separate our body spaces as women, men, children, that we sometimes have to live at the expense of others, but that this cost must be deliberately incurred and shared. In Hebrew thought redemption, as I have already remarked earlier, means giving space, being without compulsion (*yasha*). Here redemption means reciprocally occupying space and giving space.

The balance of power in our society is still engraved on our bodies. But every movement, every moving idea that is contributed to us by our skin, which limits us as women and arms us as men, can bring us nearer to such reality.

Towards a theology of embodiment

A theology of embodiment does not seek to outline a new theology, but it does seek to open up a forgotten place which is important today, from which there can be theological thought and action: the human body. It seeks to draw attention to our origin, to the fact that we are born from mothers, a fact which is constantly forgotten in a culture of fathers but which shapes us all our lives, whether we are women or men.

Stimulated by feminist praxis and theory and by feminist theology, it sees that the human body is repressed and misused in the Western Christian tradition. As woman's body it has been despised, feared, burned. Woman's full personhood has been denied her on the basis of her body. Even now it does not fit into the structures of churches and societies. The man's body has been glorified, made a norm, instrumentalized and also misused. Even now its alleged continuity shapes our ideal of the body and our understanding of achievement.

There have been signs of the return of the body for years. In the meantime experiences and investigations have shown how impressively the human body reproduces our experience, our history, our suffering, which remain stamped on it and are hard to heal. Torture, rape, incest and sexual abuse are at present the most striking examples.

The body is the place where many contemporary social and psychological processes are articulated. It is striking for church and theology how much negation and thus loss of energy can be noted in the human body.

A theology of embodiment is leading to a new interest in the bodies and lives of the most varied marginalized groups: women, the old, lesbians, homosexuals, people of colour, who have to fight for recognition in a variety of forms, and who thus suffer a loss of energy and cannot contribute their positive powers to society, since young people and white males are still favoured not only in society but also in the church.

A theological return to embodiment recalls the distinctive feature of Christianity, that God became body and in so doing has confirmed and healed all our bodily nature. This was a scandal in the religions of the ancient world – and is an unresolved challenge in the present world.

Reflection on embodiment as a central Christian topic prompts mistrust of a Western Augustinian theology which begins with the fall instead of creation and the pleasure which God took in this creation. It does not see sin as a general fate which is suffered as a matter of principle, and which for many theological traditions is still rooted in sinful human flesh, in the structure of its drives. It does not fail to recognize the potential for destruction in human beings, but sees this far more strongly as the problem of a lack of relationship, beginning in an earlier phase of life, a lack of relationship between human beings, between human beings and animals, between human beings and their environment. Sin must be made clear and identified in particular, different conflicts.

A theology of embodiment mistrusts all abstract spirituality which is dissociated from the body, life, earth and social relationships. It trusts all embodiment which speaks from a concrete, involved spirit, moved by eros and related to the cosmos. Disembodiment is lovelessness. Insecurity, coldness, power and weariness are hidden behind abstraction.

A theology of embodiment mistrusts all self-made fantasies of the beyond which are engaged in at the expense of the healing of people here and the realization of the kingdom of God on this earth. It is committed to a this-worldly expectation which here already looks for full, complete life, for wide spaces for women and men, and from this work derives the hope that nothing can separate us from the life and love of God.

It seeks to give people once again the courage to use their senses, which atrophy in a rational culture, to stand by themselves and their experiences and accept themselves with their bodies, to love them, to trust them and their understanding, and to see themselves as children of this earth, indissolubly bound up with it.

It prefers a concrete body language which also incorporates symbols, myths and fairy tales into theological discourse to a disembodied language. Instead of the traditional forensic language of salvation it seeks biblical images new and old, of being saved, becoming whole, ideas of the bodily world which correspond to the body and its rhythms and awaken healing energies in human beings which bind them to one another. It attempts to revive old rituals which affect the body and shape new ones which draw us into the cosmic dance.

However, a theology of embodiment is not in love with success. It looks at the cross as a symbol of failure, but also of a hope which is contained in the beams which point to the four corners of heaven, a hope that there is life in death, gain in failure, resurrection in passing away. For it the cross is not a symbol of Christ's sacrificial death, but a symbol of his death for a just cause.

It thinks in processes which correspond better to our life and its constant changes than linear patterns and the belief in unique and final experiences.

It is orientated on Jesus' humanity, his life, his love, his sacrifice, his passion. It regards his divinity as his deepest humanity. It discovers the God of the Bible in many images of the biblical and post-biblical tradition which are sometimes unknown even now: the woman giving birth, the beloved, the old woman, wisdom, source, tree, light.

It sees that God weeps with us and in us, for his ravaged creation and in it.

It recognizes God in many human experiences which remind us that life begins in the mother's body, that it begins as a twosome, not alone, and that our bodily life represents God's life on this earth.

'The end of all God's works is embodiment', wrote the Württemberg theologian Friedrich Christoph Oetinger in the eighteenth century. I would like to expand the sentence:

The beginning and end of all God's works is embodiment.

Bibliography

Alves, Rubem A., *I Believe in the Resurrection of the Body*, Minneapolis 1986

Bach, Ulrich, 'Wer hat Angst vor Frau N?', *Diakonia* 4, 1987

Beauvoir, Simone de, *Old Age*, London 1972

Belkina, Marija, *Die letzten Jahre der Marina Zwetajewa*, Frankfurt 1993

Berner-Hürbin, Annie, *Eros, die subtile Energie*, Basel 1989

Buytendijk, F. J. J., *Die Frau*, Cologne 1953

Böhme, Gernot, *Für eine ökologische Naturästhetik*, Frankfurt 1989

Capra, Fritjof, *Turning Point*, London 1982

Cardinal, Marie, *Schattenmund*, Reinbek 1979

Chicago, Judy, *The Dinner Party*, New York 1979

David, Janina, 'Touch of Earth', in *Square of Sky and Touch of Earth*, Harmondsworth 1981

Dinnerstein, Dorothy, *The Rocking of the Cradle and the Ruling of the World*, London 1978

Duden, Barbara, *Der Frauenleib als öffentlicher Ort*, Hamburg 1991

Gössmann, Elisabeth, 'Sinne, Seele Geist', in Pissarek-Hudelist and Schottroff (eds.), *Mit allen Sinnen glauben*, Gütersloh 1991

Goldenberg, Naomi, 'Spiritualität und Thealogie', in M. Kassel (ed.), *Feministische Theologie. Perspektiven zur Orientierung*, Stuttgart 1988.

Griffin, Susan, *Woman and Nature. The Roaring Inside Her*, New York 1978 and London 1984

Groult, Benoîte, *Salt on Our Skin*, Harmondsworth 1993

Hardach-Pinke, Irene, 'Schwangerschaft und Identität', in Kamper and Wulf, *Die Wiederkehr des Körpers*, Frankfurt 1982

Haug, Figga, *Sexualisierung der Körper*, Hamburg 1983

Henley, Nancy M., *Body Politics: Power, Sex and Nonverbal Communication*, New York 1987

Heyward, Carter, *Our Passion for Justice: Images of Power, Sexuality and Liberation*, New York 1984

Hollenweger, Walter, *Erfahrungen der Leibhaftigkeit*, Munich 1979

Illich, Ivan, *Limits to Medicine: Medical Nemesis*, London 1976

Jensen, Anne, *Gottes selbstbewusste Töchter*, Freiburg 1992

Kamper and Wulf, *Die Wiederkehr des Körpers*, Frankfurt 1982

id., *Das Schwinden der Sinne*, Frankfurt 1984

Keller, Catherine, *Penelope verlässt Odysseus*, Gütersloh 1994

Keller, Evelyn Fox, *Reflections on Gender and Science*, New Haven 1986

Krieg and Weder, *Leiblichkeit, Theologische Studien*, Zurich 1983

Lebert, Norbert, 'Der Mann', *Brigitte* 14, 1982

Lippe, Rudolf zur, *Von Leib zum Körper*, Reinbek 1988

Meyer-Abich, Klaus, *Wege zum Frieden mit der Natur*, Munich 1984

Möhrmann and Wurzbach, *Krankheit als Lebenserfahrung*, Frankfurt 1988

Moltmann, Jürgen, *God in Creation*, London and Minneapolis 1985

Moltmann-Wendel, Elisabeth (ed.), *Frau und Religion. Gotteserfahrungen im Patriarchat*, Frankfurt 1983

id., *Wenn Gott und Körper sich begegnen*, Gütersloh 1989

Montagu, Ashley, 'Die Haut', in Kamper and Wulf, *Das Schwinden der Sinne*, Frankfurt 1984

Morgan, Robin, *Anatomy of Freedom*, New York 1983

Morley, Janet, *Celebrating Women*, London 1986

Moser, Tilmann, *Grammatik der Gefühle*, Frankfurt 1979

Olbricht, Ingrid, *Die Brust*, Reinbek 1989

Olivier, Christiane, *Jocasta's Children. The Imprint of the Mother*, London 1989

Pagels, Elaine, *Adam, Eve and the Serpent*, Harmondsworth 1990

Petzold, Hilarion (ed.), *Leiblichkeit*, Paderborn 1985

Plessner, Helmuth, *Die Stufen der Organischen und der Mensch*, Berlin 1975

Praetorius, Ina, 'Die kleine Unterschied zwischen Mutter und Retorte', in *Frauen für eine gerechte Sprache*, Gütersloh 1990

Rohr, Richard, *Der nackte Gott*, Munich 1988

id., *Der wilde Mann*, Munich 1992

Rose, Lotte, 'Körper ohne Raum', *Feministische Studien* 1992.1, Weinheim 1992

Rousselle, Aline, *Der Ursprung der Keuschheit*, Stuttgart 1989

Ruether, Rosemary Radford, *Sexism and God-Talk*, Boston and London 1983

Schnack and Neutzling, *Kleine Helden in Not*, Reinbek 1992

Schweizer, Eduard, *Good News according to Mark*, Atlanta 1974

Seybold and Müller, *Krankheit und Heilung*, Stuttgart 1978

Sheehy, Gail, *Passages*, Toronto 1976

Steinem, Gloria, *Revolution from Within*, Boston 1987

Stopcyk, Annegret, *Leibphilosophie*, Manuscript, Saarland Rundfunk 1991: obtainable from Forderkreis Sophia-Leibphilosophie, c/o Monika Waldmüller, Alban Stolz Strasse 22, 7918 Freiburg, Germany

Sturm, Vilma, *Alte Tage*, Munich 1988

Sullerot, Evelyne, *Die Wirklichkeit der Frau*, Munich 1979

Trummer, Peter, *Die blutende Frau*, Freiburg 1991

Wander, Maxie, *Guten Morgen, du Schöne*, Darmstadt 1978

Ead., *Leben wär' eine prima Alternativa*, Darmstadt 1980

Warner, Marina, *Monuments and Maidens*, London 1985

Weder, Hans, in Krieg and Weder, *Leiblichkeit, Theologische Studien*, Zurich 1983

Wendebourg, Dorothea, 'Die alttestamentlischen Reinheitsgesetze in der frühen Kirche', *Zeitschrift für Kirchengeschichte* 1984.2, Stuttgart 1984

Weizsäcker, Viktor von, *Der Lebenskreis*, Stuttgart 1950

Wilson Schaef, Anne, *Women's Reality: An Emerging Female System in a White Male Society*, New York 1985